CLUTTERED MESS TO
ORGANIZED SUCCESS

WORKBOOK

**Declutter & Organize Your Home and Life
with over 100 Checklists and Worksheets
+ Free Full Downloads**

Cassandra Aarssen

For permission requests, please contact the publisher at:

Mango Publishing Group
2850 Douglas Road, 3rd Floor
Coral Gables, FL 33134 U.S.A.
info@mango.bz

For special orders, quantity sales, course adoptions and corporate sales, please email the publisher at sales@mango.bz. For trade and wholesale sales, please contact Ingram Publisher Services at customer. service@ingramcontent.com or +1.800.509.4887.

Cluttered Mess to Organized Success: Declutter & Organize Your Home and Life with over 100 Checklists and Worksheets + Free Full Downloads

Library of Congress Cataloging
ISBN: (print) 978-1-63353-708-8, (ebook) 978-1-63353-709-5
Library of Congress Control Number: 2017915646
BISAC HOUSE & HOME / Cleaning, Caretaking & Organizing
Code: HOM019000

Printed in the United States of America

Alice, this book is for you and because of you.

I'm so thankful for having you in my life.

Table of Contents

CHAPTER THREE: ORGANIZING YOUR FAMILY   55

HOW TO DECLUTTER YOUR BRAIN AND MAKE FAMILY LIFE EASIER.

CHAPTER FOUR: ORGANIZING YOUR HOME   73

HOW TO GET YOUR HOME CLEAN AND CLUTTER-FREE.

CHAPTER FIVE: ORGANIZING YOUR MEALS

HOW TO SAVE TIME, MONEY, AND EAT HEALTHIER WITH MEAL PLANNING.

≋ Introduction ≋

CLUTTERED MESS TO ORGANIZED SUCCESS

A REAL LIFE APPROACH TO DECLUTTERING AND TIDYING-UP YOUR HOME.

Hi, my name is Cassandra Aarssen, and I am a recovering super-slob. Not only was my home insanely cluttered, but my *life* was a cluttered mess as well. After years of struggling and drowning in clutter (both the physical and mental kind) my life has been totally transformed through a few simple organizing solutions. For all intents and purposes, I finally have this whole "adult" thing pretty much figured out. I can't wait to share my secrets with you!

If you are reading this book, chances are you are looking to infuse a little bit of organization into your life. I can promise you that if you take the time to complete the worksheets, do the checklists and use the labels included in this book, you will be catapulted from a cluttered mess to an organized success, no matter what your situation is right now. How can I be so confident in my claim? This book is the exact recipe I used for my own organizational success—and I was a hot mess.

This book is going to be a little different than your traditional, organizational self-help book. It's more of an instructional manual for how to declutter and organize your home and your entire life. I'm going to walk you through the complete process of organizing your time, home, finances, and even your dreams and aspirations in life. Taking just a few minutes to write down and make a plan for your biggest and most ambitious dreams is exactly how they are going to become a reality. This book can help you achieve the life that you deserve!

"IF YOU FAIL TO PLAN, YOU ARE PLANNING TO FAIL!"
—BENJAMIN FRANKLIN

This workbook is about more than having a clean and clutter-free home (though we will make a plan for this as well); **it's about creating your life plan**. This little workbook you are reading is going to help you transform every aspect of your life, from reducing your stress to increasing your overall happiness. I am thrilled to guide you on your journey towards an organized and decluttered life.

I've made it my mission to help other families break free from their clutter. This desire to help comes from my own battle with chronic disorganization. I've struggled for years in vain to get my life together, so I know first hand what a devastating impact our physical space can have on our health and happiness. I want to share all the tips and secrets I've learned, which have helped me achieve a life free from stress and clutter and full of success and happiness.

I have always struggled with the very basic of life skills. I was almost certainly diagnosed with ADHD, but at the time, ADHD wasn't widely known, let alone diagnosed (yeah, I'm that old). As a kid, I struggled to pay attention and was insanely hyper. I also had zero impulse control, which meant I got in trouble, **a lot**. I literally spent my entire grade six school year with my desk sitting in the hallway, just so the rest of the class could get work done. **The mental skills that help you control impulses, focus, and accomplish tasks are called "Executive Function" and are controlled by your prefrontal cortex**. Research has shown that children and adults suffering from ADHD have slightly smaller and less active prefrontal cortexes, breaking the myth that this diagnosis is made up or that it is something that can be *cured* with medication or discipline. My prefrontal cortex must be super duper tiny.

My dad used to tell me that I "*walked to the beat of my own drum,*" which I'm pretty sure is just a polite way of calling me a total weirdo. Despite my parents' best efforts, my lack of self-control wreaked havoc on my teenage years and I continued to struggle well into my late twenties. While my friends were all graduating from college and university, I was struggling to keep my random minimum wage jobs for more than just a few months at a time. My apartment looked like an episode from *Hoarders* and my bank account was overdrawn more often than it wasn't.

I was **that** person. You know the kind I'm talking about. I was the person who was always late for everything (if I even remembered to show up in the first place). I could never find my car keys, or my purse...or my cell phone, and I just always seemed *frantic*. After I became a stay-at-home mom, my scattered brain and lack of household management skills were magnified and I was completely overwhelmed and depressed.

My glaring mom fails were made **super** apparent every morning that I braved the dreaded school drop-off line. While the other moms (with their perky ponytails and Lululemon pants) were leisurely kissing their kids goodbye, I was the mom tumbling out of her filthy mini van in her wrinkled PJs while screaming for her kids to **run**. Not only did we miss the school bus every day (forcing me to face the Lulu moms at the drop-off line in all my dishevelled glory), most of the time, we didn't even make it before the bell rang. I wasn't only making my own life more difficult and stressful, my complete lack of organization was impacting my entire family. Something needed to change. I needed to change.

Today, as an organizing expert, I am able to help hundreds of thousands of busy families transform their lives through planning, decluttering, and organization. Organizing hasn't just become my passion; it has become my thriving and fast-growing business called ClutterBug. I am so grateful to be able to do what I love and help other hot-mess mommies through my YouTube channel, blog, podcast, and best-selling book *Real Life Organizing* (shameless plug). My organizing advice has even been featured on national television shows, magazines, news outlets, and hundreds of blogs and websites all over the world (even Oprah.com...I know, right?). The irony of my newfound career has not escaped me.

So what changed? How did I go from never having clean underwear to becoming an organizational expert? The truth is, I still suffer from mild ADHD, but I have learned to manage my lack of Executive Function (a.k.a. *internal* organization) through easy **external** organizing solutions.

It started with a small and easy change; I started *planning* my life. The very first plan I ever made was a simple list of the household chores. I put this list on the fridge and forced myself to check off as many items as I could.

My plans were not elaborate or even well thought out at first. I'm pretty sure I used a scrap piece of paper and never even accomplished half of what I had written on those lists. **It was just the simple act of making plans in the first place that gave me direction and a purpose that I never had before.** That was it. That was the catalyst for my life's transformation. Just some scrap pieces of paper and a pen were all I needed to create the organizing processes that I had been so sorely lacking. **Implementing those plans took time and practice, but it was having the plan written down in the first place that made all the difference.** I created my own "Executive Function," prefrontal cortex be damned. Whether you are also suffering from ADHD, or you just need a little extra help creating organizing systems in your life, I am positive this approach can have the exact same effect on you as it did for me. So, let's set the world on fire! Who needs a stinkin' match when you have a plan?

> FOR TOMORROW BELONGS TO THOSE WHO PREPARE FOR IT TODAY.
> —MALCOLM X

HOW TO USE THIS BOOK:

Write in it! Don't be afraid to fill in the pages, cut them out, and try the different checklists and worksheets to see what works for you and what doesn't. If you decide to cut out the worksheets and labels directly from this book, just remember that there are other sheets on the backside of each page. You can also print out all of the pages in this book, along with some bonus pages, as part of your free instant download (just in case you would rather leave this book intact).

This book isn't for sitting on your coffee table and looking pretty—this book is a tool for transforming your life. Get it dirty, write in it, cut it up and don't feel bad about it for a second.

Don't forget...all of the beautiful pages in this book are available to you as a free instant download printable pack. **Simply visit www.clutterbug.me/ClutteredMess and use the code: "success" to receive your digital copies emailed directly to you.**

Chapter One

ORGANIZING YOUR GOALS & DREAMS

HOW TO MAKE YOUR GOALS AND DREAMS COME TRUE.

I think there is a misconception that goal-setting is some overwhelming or monumental task that needs a lot of time and effort to accomplish. The truth is, we already set multiple goals for ourselves each and every day, without even thinking about it. Waking up on time, making our bed, or eating a healthy breakfast are all common daily goals that most of us already share (we may not always achieve these goals every day, but they are goals nonetheless).

What I want to help you do in this chapter is **organize** your goals and really focus on the bigger, more life-changing ones. I want you to use the goal-setting worksheets on the next few pages to pick a dream and create a plan to make that dream a reality. **This is much easier to do than you think; the simple act of writing down your dream instantly makes it a goal.** Once you break that goal down into smaller goals and give yourself a timeline to complete them, you now have a plan. Once you have a plan, it's simply a matter of organizing your time to include your plan into your daily or weekly schedule. Now you have an attainable action plan. Taking action on your plan is exactly how you will make all of your wildest dreams come true.

⫸

A DREAM IS JUST A DREAM. A GOAL IS A DREAM WITH A PLAN.

⫷

Once you have your goals and plan in place, it is time for the implementation process (a.k.a. getting shit done). The best and most efficient way to make sure you get things done is to make yourself a to-do list each and every day. Achieving any goal, big or small, requires breaking that goal down into small, achievable steps.

>>>

THIS IS WHY A SIMPLE TO-DO LIST IS ONE OF THE MOST LIFE-CHANGING ORGANIZATIONAL TOOLS YOU WILL EVER USE.

<<<

I was never a list maker before. My mom was an avid list maker and it drove me bonkers as a kid. Perhaps in quiet rebellion, I was fundamentally against making lists for myself. I mean, it seemed ridiculous to have to make a list for the things that I already knew I had to do each day. I already had a mental list, am I right?

Unfortunately, it's not only that I have the memory of a hamster; my lack of daily to-do lists meant that I suffered from a chronic lack of motivation. **That is truly the magic of list making—the motivation they create.** Nothing is more motivating than checking off the item you've completed. It gives you a sense of accomplishment, transforming that motivation into momentum to keep going.

>>>

A SIMPLE DAILY TO-DO LIST IS GOING TO TRANSFORM YOUR PRODUCTIVITY. IF I HAD TO PINPOINT JUST ONE THING THAT HAS HAD THE GREATEST IMPACT ON MY LIFE, MY DAILY TO-DO LISTS WOULD BE IT.

<<<

After years of reading countless self-help books that all basically said the exact same thing (pick a goal and make a plan), I finally took some of that advice and wrote down a dream for myself. **My first ever, big-girl dream? To become a stay-at-home mom.** For me to achieve this, I needed to replace the income from my full-time career and create a job that would earn me the same amount of income while I worked from home.

I started by writing down my dream: be a stay-at-home mom, and then my goal: earn a full-time income from home. I had to calculate how much income I would need to bring in (minus the daycare costs I would be saving) in order to make my goal a reality. Once I had a clear goal, I made a list of all the potential money-earning options I could try. This was, of course, my plan. I tried...and failed...at a lot of those various plans before finding one that worked.

Some of my "work from home" plans were so absolutely ridiculous and others, while they seemed great on paper, just didn't work out. I tried selling homemade jewelry, hair bows, and tutus through my Etsy shop, but the income just wasn't enough to replace my current salary. I tried a few different multi-level marketing sales jobs, but I wasn't comfortable selling products to strangers because, well, **people** make me anxious. I worked as a home stager and a house cleaner, but clients wanted me to work during the day, which meant I couldn't be with my kids (defeating the purpose entirely). I even tried being a clown...for **reals**. I tried starting a **birthday party clown** business for weekend birthday parties where I would dress up in a clown costume, tell jokes, and make balloon animals. Apparently, I'm just not that funny. Eventually I started a successful home-based daycare that allowed me to be home with my children while giving them many wonderful friends to play with and earning me a full-time income at the same time.

I'm constantly creating new goals and plans, and despite never achieving all of them, I have learned how important—no, **imperative**—this process is for success in all areas of my life.

Whether your dream is to have a clean and organized home, financial freedom, or to start your own business, the steps to achieving all of these dreams are exactly the same. So write down your dream and let's start planning for it right now! The sky is the limit for your potential, so dream big, my friend.

Take a few minutes to fill out the following pages. Don't overthink it, you can always revise or redo it later. **This isn't about being perfect or having it all figured out right now, this is about making the first step towards your future, more amazeballs self.**

You can find some example goal-setting sheets already filled out in this chapter, which hopefully will help make your own goal-setting much easier. Once you are done creating your dream action plan and to-do lists, make sure that you schedule yourself time to work on your goals when you create your daily, weekly, and monthly schedules in the next chapter.

So, let's get started! Here are some worksheets to help you get into gear. Create your own goals and plans using these tools!

❧ Goal-setting ❧

YOUR DREAM

STEPPING STONES TO SUCCESS

Fill in the circles below with the goals you need to accomplish your dream.

PRIORITIZE

Choose three of your goals that you want to achieve first.

 GOAL ONE

 GOAL TWO

 GOAL THREE

Goal-setting

An organized home

STEPPING STONES TO SUCCESS

Fill in the circles below with the goals you need to accomplish your dream.

Organized kitchen	Clutter-free home	Organized bedroom	A place for shoes
Paper filling system	Organized bathroom	More storage	Organized garage

PRIORITIZE

Choose three of your goals that you want to achieve first.

GOAL ONE

Organized kitchen

GOAL TWO

Clutter-free home

GOAL THREE

More storage

Goal Action Planner

GOAL: _____

_____

ACTION TO TAKE:

☐ _____
☐ _____
☐ _____
☐ _____
☐ _____

DUE DATE: _____   ☐ I DID IT! _____

GOAL: _____

_____

ACTION TO TAKE:

☐ _____
☐ _____
☐ _____
☐ _____
☐ _____

DUE DATE: _____   ☐ I DID IT! _____

If you can dream it, you can do it.

Goal Action Planner

JAN – FEB – (MAR) – APR – MAY – JUNE
JULY – AUG – SEPT – OCT – NOV – DEC

GOAL: Organized kitchen

ACTION TO TAKE:
- ☐ Donate unused items
- ☐ Buy containers
- ☐ Organize pantry
- ☐ Clean and organize fridge and freezer
- ☐ Organize cabinets and drawers

DUE DATE: March 31st   ☑ I DID IT!

JAN – FEB – (MAR) – APR – MAY – JUNE
JULY – AUG – SEPT – OCT – NOV – DEC

GOAL: Clutter-free home

ACTION TO TAKE:
- ☐ Clear surfaces
- ☐ Purge 21 items each week for one month
- ☐ Create new homes for "homeless clutter"
- ☐ Donate 21 items from my closet
- ☐ Purchase new shelving unit for family room

DUE DATE: March 30th   ☑ I DID IT!

If you can dream it, you can do it.

Everyday
DO SOMETHING THAT WILL
inch you closer
TO A BETTER
Tomorrow.

❧ Creating a Plan ❧
IDENTIFY YOUR GOAL AND MAKE A PLAN TO ACHIEVE IT

AREA TO FOCUS ON:

_____

_____

WHY IS THIS AREA IMPORTANT TO FOCUS ON?

_____

_____

WHAT IS EFFECTIVE?

_____

_____

_____

WHAT IS NOT EFFECTIVE?

_____

_____

_____

LIST OF TASKS, RESPONSIBILITIES, AND IDEAS TO IMPROVE THIS AREA:

_____

_____

_____

_____

_____

_____

_____

_____

❧ Short Term Goal ❧

GOAL:	DUE DATE:

Details and Specifics

HOW AM I GETTING THERE?

Actions to Take	Due Date:	

❧ Long Term Goal ❧

GOAL:	DUE DATE:

Details and Specifics

WHAT NEEDS TO BE DONE FIRST?

Supportive Short Term Goals	Due Date:	

Goals For The Week

ME:

HONEY DO LIST:

Monthly Dreams and Goals

TAKE A MINUTE TO MAKE YOURSELF
SOME GOALS OVER THE NEXT YEAR!

JANUARY

FEBRUARY

MARCH

APRIL

MAY

JUNE

Monthly Dreams and Goals

TAKE A MINUTE TO MAKE YOURSELF
SOME GOALS OVER THE NEXT YEAR!

JULY

AUGUST

SEPTEMBER

OCTOBER

NOVEMBER

DECEMBER

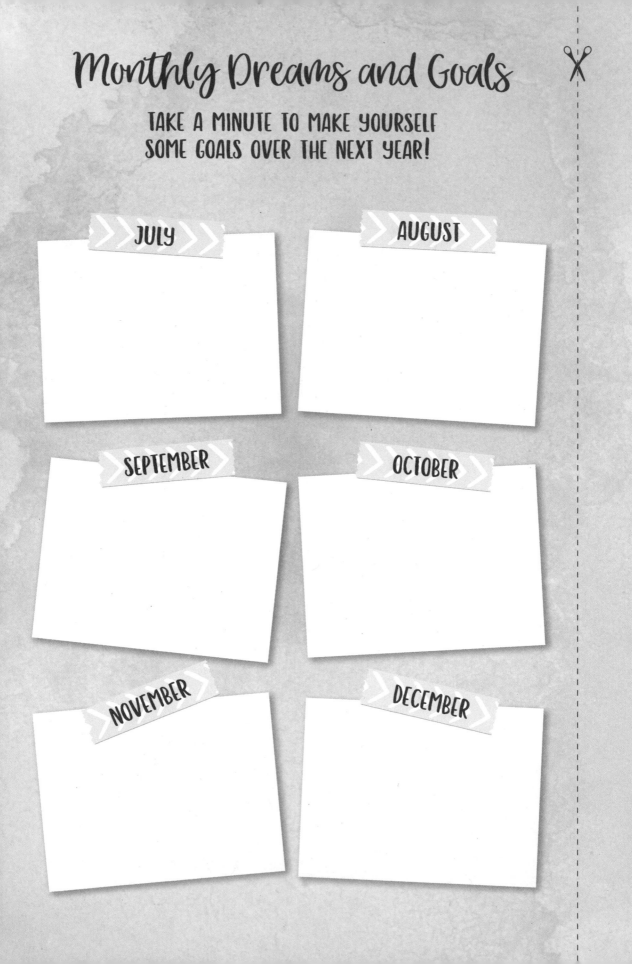

Small Goals

SET SOME SMALL GOALS FOR YOURSELF THAT YOU CAN ACCOMPLISH IN JUST ONE DAY!

Examples: Paint your bathroom, organize your junk drawer, send a card to a loved one.

RESOLUTION	ACHIEVED BY	ACHIEVED
		YES ○ NO ○
		YES ○ NO ○
		YES ○ NO ○
		YES ○ NO ○
		YES ○ NO ○
		YES ○ NO ○
		YES ○ NO ○
		YES ○ NO ○
		YES ○ NO ○
		YES ○ NO ○
		YES ○ NO ○
		YES ○ NO ○
		YES ○ NO ○
		YES ○ NO ○
		YES ○ NO ○
		YES ○ NO ○
		YES ○ NO ○
		YES ○ NO ○
		YES ○ NO ○
		YES ○ NO ○
		YES ○ NO ○
		YES ○ NO ○
		YES ○ NO ○

Wake up and Shine

≋ Chapter Two ≋

ORGANIZING YOUR TIME

HOW TO GET MORE DONE IN LESS TIME.

"YOU WILL NEVER FIND TIME FOR ANYTHING. IF YOU WANT TIME, YOU MUST MAKE IT."
—CHARLES BUXTON

We are all *"busy."* We live in a world filled with appointments, deadlines, and a never-ending parade of things we need to accomplish. For me, I was stuck in this perpetual state of "rushing" for the longest time, without any real sense of what I was rushing towards. Can anyone else totally relate to Alabama's song "I'm In A Hurry"? Seriously, that was the theme song for my entire life.

With three little kids, a home-based business, and all the household responsibilities that come with adulting, I have a lot on my plate. I spent the better part of ten years in a blur of work, kids, and household chores, and I wasn't managing any of those things particularly well. I was always so stressed out about all the things I had to do each day that I wasn't actually accomplishing very much of it at all. I'm pretty sure I spent most of my time fretting about my hectic life and procrastinating on actually getting anything productive done. I would rush around doing small, silly tasks, all the while completely avoiding the things that would have the biggest impact on my life. I call this "ostriching" because it's basically the equivalent of sticking my head in the sand whenever I feel overwhelmed—as if ignoring the things I had to get done would somehow make them disappear.

I still have not completely mastered the art of time management or productivity. In all honesty, I really, kind of, suck at it. While I could definitely get way more done in a day, I certainly have come a long way in the past two years. I grew my online business to over 300,000 combined followers, created new revenue streams through multiple platforms that allow me to earn a great income, and I even wrote a best-selling book (yeah, I'm tooting my own horn for a second). I am now able to accomplish more than I ever thought possible and I have way more free time than I ever did before. The difference? **I started scheduling and organizing my time.**

>>>

THE TRICK TO GETTING MORE DONE IN LESS TIME IS TO ORGANIZE YOUR SCHEDULE AHEAD OF TIME.

<<<

Taking just a few minutes to schedule your day can save you hours of wasted time and send your productivity through the roof. **Even if you are like me and you don't accomplish everything you had planned on getting done, you are still going to be way more productive than you ever would be without having a schedule in the first place**.

Just writing it down makes you more likely to accomplish it. Organizing and scheduling your time will equal more productivity and overall success. I know, it's a bold claim, but it's one that I can back up with my own personal experience and from the personal experiences of all the successful people I know. My friends and family who seem to have it all together have this one thing in common: they make managing and organizing their time a priority. Take a minute to think about the people in your own life who seem to accomplish so much more than the average person. I can promise you that they all make it a priority to plan and organize their time in order to achieve their super boss status.

When it comes to organizing your time, it's not just about writing your appointments, meetings, and birthdays into your daily planner or calendar. While this is an important step, you really need to go deeper into time management in order to see a big impact on your life.

≫

THE SECRET OF GOOD TIME MANAGEMENT IS TO PLAN YOUR TASKS, PRIORITIZE THEM, AND THEN ORGANIZE THOSE TASKS INTO YOUR DAILY, WEEKLY, AND MONTHLY SCHEDULES.

≪

I used to resist the idea of having a daily routine and schedule because I felt like it would stifle my creativity or make my life mundane. The idea of having schedules and routines felt like conformity, when in reality, it was really about maturity. The truth is, organizing my time properly has opened up my life and given me much more time for the things I truly love. A daily, monthly, and even yearly schedule has given me freedom, not confinement, and it can do the same thing for you.

So where do you start? How can you transform your life and get more done each day and have more free time for yourself than ever before? **You start with your morning and night-time routine.** Great mornings equal great days. String those great days together and you end up with a really great life. Having a morning routine is so important because it really sets the tone for your entire day. A great morning routine is a game changer when it comes to your positivity and your productivity.

So, let's talk about some simple ways you can make your mornings amazing. Simply by scheduling a few quick and easy tasks each morning, you can improve your outlook, productivity and overall happiness. I want to you to schedule yourself some time each morning to do a few small things that will improve your day and bring you joy.

Your routine should include a few things that you have always wanted to make more time for in your life, but can never really find the time. Your routine should also be realistic. At first, I planned to take the dog for a walk every morning and make myself a protein shake, I could just never stick with it. I failed miserably every morning, which had the opposite effect that I was going for. Instead, I picked easy things that I LOVED doing, not just things I thought I was "supposed" to do. Your morning routine is where you make time, even if for only 10–15 minutes, for the things that bring you joy (no, sleeping in does not count).

HERE IS MY MORNING ROUTINE:

- **Drink a big glass of water (1 minute)**
- **Read comments and messages from my amazing followers (20 minutes)**
- **Plan my day while listening to my favorite podcast (15 minutes)**
- **Get ready (30 minutes)**
- **Make my bed (5 minutes)**

My morning routine takes me a grand total of 71 minutes. I used to forgo all except the getting ready part, which did give me an extra bit of sleep each morning, but I started my day rushed, hectic, and feeling like I wanted to crawl back into bed. Now that I set my alarm for 40 minutes earlier, I get to spend that time doing things that not only make me happy, but make me feel energized as well.

Drinking a big glass of water as soon as I wake up makes me instantly feel more awake and the fact that it is good for me is just an added bonus. I literally drink a glass of water each morning before I even get out of bed. This is one of those things that even a lazy person like me can work into their routine!

Next, I spend some time reading messages and comments from my subscribers. This makes me crazy happy! I'm so blessed to be able to wake up to messages filled with such love and support each and every day.

After filling my heart with happiness from all the kind messages, I make tea and have breakfast. Every day I plan to eat a healthy breakfast, but hey man, no one is perfect. Breakfast is usually sugary, carby junk (so yummy), but I listen to a podcast or an audiobook while I eat, which again, makes me so happy. I also use this time to fill out my daily action planner page (found in this chapter) to organize my day. What do I *need* to get done? What do I *want* to get done? I plan everything from my work schedule, kids activities, errands, meals and housework during this time.

Lastly, I get ready for the day and make my bed. The really important part of this routine is the fact that I have made time for joyful and productive activities as soon as I wake up. Once I'm ready for the day, then I wake up the kids. Here is the craziest part; when I get them up for school and I'm in a happy and energized mood, **they** wake up in a happier mood as well! Busy school mornings go much smoother and I no longer end up screaming for them to "hurry up and put on your shoes" as we race out the door to catch the bus.

Not only does my morning routine make me feel more awake and optimistic, but my positive attitude transfers to my family and carries with us for the rest of my day.

Sound too good to be true? Try it for yourself! Design yourself a daily morning routine right now. Remember to include things that will make you feel happy. These may include meditation, journaling, yoga, reading a book, going for a walk, making breakfast or having coffee with a loved one. Set your alarm clock 30–45 minutes earlier than you would normally get up and use that time just for you—doing things that bring you joy.

You may not be a morning person and I can one hundred percent relate. I am a night owl, so I resisted the idea of getting up earlier in the morning. I love sleeping in and I need at least eight hours sleep or I feel exhausted come lunchtime. **The thing is, I couldn't argue with the results.** The first day I dragged myself out of bed earlier and did my morning routine, I felt *incredible*. I was shocked by how great I felt and even more shocked at how much more productive I was the entire day. Here is the secret for us "non-morning people." In order for me to have a successful morning routine, I needed to create a night-time routine first.

I am pretty sure my night-time routine may be even **more** important than my morning one. It doesn't have the same euphoric impact on my mood, but without it, my morning routine just isn't happening. I need to take a few minutes each night to get set up for the next morning because planning is half the battle.

HERE IS MY NIGHT-TIME ROUTINE:

- **Clean kitchen (10 minutes)**
- **Tidy up clutter (5 minutes)**
- **Spot wipe main bathroom (5 minutes)**
- **Set out daily action planner and pen (1 minute)**
- **Set out clothing for next day (1 minute)**
- **Put glass of water on bedside table (1 minute)**

Because of my nightly schedule, I get to wake up each morning to a clean and tidy home (which instantly makes me feel good) and I have everything I need ready and waiting for me. I'm groggy in the morning and this makes me lazy. Because everything I need to accomplish my morning routine is already set out and ready to go, I have no excuse! I wake up feeling happy and prepared and it is all because I took just 23 minutes before bed to get organized for the next day.

≫

SO, FILL OUT THE MORNING AND EVENING ROUTINE WORKSHEET AND WATCH THE MAGIC HAPPEN!

≪

In this chapter, you are also going to find amazing planning pages to help you organize and schedule your time better. **I've included many different monthly and daily planner page styles, so you can choose the one that best fits your needs.** Start with the monthly planners to organize your time by scheduling time for your goals, appointments, birthdays, and other main tasks and activities. Use the weekly and daily planners to get more detailed with your time management and really breakdown your schedule into small, manageable tasks.

≫

I RECOMMEND PRIORITIZING YOUR DAILY TASKS AND ALWAYS DOING THE MOST IMPORTANT TASK FIRST!

≪

This prioritizing technique is called "Eat That Frog" and is really effective in combatting procrastination. I first read this concept a few years ago in a best-selling book by the same name. The basic theory was based on a quote by Mark Twain which stated, **"If the first thing you do each morning is to eat a live frog, you can go through the day with the satisfaction of knowing that that is probably the worst thing that is going to happen to you all day long."** Basically, what this means is, if you complete the worst and most dreaded task on your list first, the rest of your day is going to seem pretty good in comparison. This is also effective because the most dreaded tasks on your list are probably the most important. When I "Eat My Frog" each morning, I never have to worry about not having enough time to get the really important stuff done.

So let's start scheduling! In my home, I have two separate monthly calendars, one for my family activities, birthdays, and events and one calendar just for my work schedule. Great time management works the exact same way, whether you are trying to accomplish more at your job, in your home or even during your free time.

Great time management starts with choosing your top three priorities for the day. Pick the three things that are your "immediate action" tasks and write down the things you need to accomplish in order to achieve those goals. Next, make a list of all the other things that require your attention and be sure to prioritize them into categories from most important to least important. **Now complete the most important tasks first, it really is as simple as that!**

Customize the following schedules, calendars and worksheets to fit you and your lifestyle. Remember, these worksheets are available for you to download for free at anytime, so don't be afraid to use these ones for practice!

Just by writing down your schedule and prioritizing your daily tasks, you will instantly be setting the foundation for your time management success!

Good Morning Routine

- [ ] _____
- [ ] _____
- [ ] _____
- [ ] _____
- [ ] _____
- [ ] _____
- [ ] _____

Good Evening Routine

- [ ] _____
- [ ] _____
- [ ] _____
- [ ] _____
- [ ] _____
- [ ] _____
- [ ] _____

Time Management Worksheet

Make the most of your workday

TOP THREE DAILY PRIORITIES

_____

_____

_____

SUPPORTIVE THINGS TO DO

CHORES YOU NEED TO ADULT TODAY

1
2
3
4
5
6
7
8
9
10

OH NO, ERRANDS!

1
2
3
4

TODAY'S APPOINTMENTS

:
:
:
:

doodle

ACTION NOW

TO DO LIST

TODAY'S GOALS

HOW HARD DID YOU WORK OUT?

What did you do? _____

8 OZ. OF WATER - HYDRATE!

EAT BALANCED HEALTHY FOODS

B
S
L
S
D

NOTES

Today

SCHEDULE:

6 A.M. _____

7 _____

8 _____

9 _____

10 _____

11 _____

12 P.M. _____

1 _____

2 _____

3 _____

4 _____

5 _____

6 _____

7 _____

8 _____

9 _____

10 _____

DATE:

_____

AFTERNOON:

_____

_____

_____

_____

_____

_____

_____

_____

_____

_____

_____

_____

MUST DO!

_____

_____

_____

_____

_____

_____

Daily Planner

DATE:

_____

PRIORITIES:

1

2

3

WORKOUT:

WATER:

● ● ● ● ● ● ● ● ● ●

MEALS:

B

L

D

S

MORNING:

_____
_____
_____
_____
_____

AFTERNOON:

_____
_____
_____
_____

EVENING:

_____
_____
_____
_____

NOTES:

It's a Beautiful Day

DATE:

TO DO:

PRIORITIES:

1

2

3

APPOINTMENTS:

:

:

:

:

:

HABITS:

MEALS:

B

L

D

S

NOTES:

Priority Planner

Prioritizing Your Day Will Help You Achieve More

MY MOST IMPORTANT TASKS AND RESPONSIBILITIES

THE OTHER IMPORTANT/URGENT THINGS THAT NEED MY ATTENTION

IF I HAVE TIME

THINGS TO DO FOR ME - PICK AT LEAST ONE PER DAY

Weekly Planner

MONDAY

TUESDAY

WEDNESDAY

THURSDAY

FRIDAY

SATURDAY

SUNDAY

My Week

MONDAY	TUESDAY	WEDNESDAY
6 A.M. _____	6 A.M. _____	6 A.M. _____
7 _____	7 _____	7 _____
8 _____	8 _____	8 _____
9 _____	9 _____	9 _____
10 _____	10 _____	10 _____
11 _____	11 _____	11 _____
12 P.M. _____	12 P.M. _____	12 P.M. _____
1 _____	1 _____	1 _____
2 _____	2 _____	2 _____
3 _____	3 _____	3 _____
4 _____	4 _____	4 _____
5 _____	5 _____	5 _____
6 _____	6 _____	6 _____
7 _____	7 _____	7 _____
8 _____	8 _____	8 _____
9 _____	9 _____	9 _____
10 _____	10 _____	10 _____

NOTES: _____

_____

_____

❧ My Week ❧

THURSDAY	FRIDAY	SATURDAY
6 A.M. _____	6 A.M. _____	_____
7 _____	7 _____	_____
8 _____	8 _____	_____
9 _____	9 _____	_____
10 _____	10 _____	_____
11 _____	11 _____	_____
12 P.M. _____	12 P.M. _____	_____
1 _____	1 _____	_____
2 _____	2 _____	**SUNDAY**
3 _____	3 _____	_____
4 _____	4 _____	_____
5 _____	5 _____	_____
6 _____	6 _____	_____
7 _____	7 _____	_____
8 _____	8 _____	_____
9 _____	9 _____	_____
10 _____	10 _____	_____

NOTES: _____
_____
_____

Monthly Planner

JANUARY

_____
_____
_____
_____
_____
_____
_____
_____

APRIL

_____
_____
_____
_____
_____
_____
_____
_____

FEBRUARY

_____
_____
_____
_____
_____
_____
_____
_____

MAY

_____
_____
_____
_____
_____
_____
_____
_____

MARCH

_____
_____
_____
_____
_____
_____
_____

JUNE

_____
_____
_____
_____
_____
_____
_____

Monthly Planner

JULY

_____
_____
_____
_____
_____
_____
_____
_____

OCTOBER

_____
_____
_____
_____
_____
_____
_____
_____

AUGUST

_____
_____
_____
_____
_____
_____
_____
_____

NOVEMBER

_____
_____
_____
_____
_____
_____
_____
_____

SEPTEMBER

_____
_____
_____
_____
_____
_____
_____
_____

DECEMBER

_____
_____
_____
_____
_____
_____
_____
_____

YOU WILL NEVER CHANGE YOUR LIFE until you change SOMETHING YOU DO DAILY. The secret of your SUCCESS is bound in your DAILY ROUTINE.

≋ Chapter Three ≋

ORGANIZING YOUR FAMILY

HOW TO DECLUTTER YOUR BRAIN AND MAKE FAMILY LIFE EASIER.

It's truth time; I'm still a hot-mess mom. Despite my best efforts, I don't completely have my life together. My kids still watch more television than they should, I've completely forgotten about dentist appointments (more than once) and we still eat take-out at least once a week. But guess what? I'm now an **organized** hot-mess mom. My kids no longer miss the school bus every day, I know where my cars keys, wallet, and phone are (most of the time) and I'm finally able to juggle my home and career life, without either of them suffering.

I thought I was managing the family schedule stuff pretty well when my kids where really little. To be honest, I remember thinking "this mom thing is a piece of cake" and wondering why so many other moms seemed so rushed and tired all the time. I mean, sure the house was messy and I could never find anything, but overall, I felt like I had some resemblance of control over our family's schedule.

Once all three of my kids were in school and involved in extra curricular activities every night of the week, well, then it was game over. I could hardly remember my own birthday, let alone anyone else's. I honestly thought I was thirty-eight for an entire year, despite just turning thirty-seven. My mind was a jumbled mess, so full of all the things I needed to remember, I couldn't seem to remember anything at all. I had a bad case of brain clutter.

ENTER THIS BOOK! HAVING LISTS AND SCHEDULES FOR MY FAMILY HAS SAVED ME FROM A TOTAL #MOMFAIL ALMOST DAILY.

With three kids in extracurricular activities, I usually spend all five weeknights playing personal chauffeur to hockey, taekwondo, power skating, and piano. Don't even get me started on our weekends! Almost every single Saturday and Sunday seems to be booked solid with birthday parties, play dates, sporting tournaments, or family gatherings.

Having school-aged children also means you have to keep track of homework assignments, field trips, hot dog days, fundraisers, book fairs, and all the other various "special" school days (crazy hair day, green day, silly hat day...you get the idea). Not to mention having to organize all of your kids' friends information. My kids have so many friends, and they all seem to end up at our house seven days a week. I need to keep track of their various food allergies and be able to contact their parents quickly and easily in case of an emergency.

Even if you don't have children, having extended family and friends still requires a lot of organization. Scheduling events, birthdays, anniversaries, holidays and keeping track of contact information can just be the beginning. I also think it's important to have the contact information for your closest neighbors, just in case of emergencies.

Thankfully, almost everyone has a phone nowadays, and we can keep track of a lot of this stuff in our phones. That being said, **I really recommend keeping a paper copy of important contact information and schedules as a backup.** I've dropped, lost, or had my phone stolen enough times to learn this lesson the hard way.

The best part of taking time to brain dump all the family stuff you have to remember onto good old fashion paper is that it becomes an organizing tool that your entire family can use. I created a binder where I put all the important information I have to remember, so that it's easy for everyone to access. This way I can share the responsibility and it's not always up to me to schedule and remember everything. I call it my "family planner" and it is awesome sauce.

My family planner alleviates so much of the pressure from my poor overworked brain. I don't have to worry about remembering the names of my kid's friend's parents or when the next parent-teacher meeting is. I can quickly call my neighbor if I need to borrow something and I have peace of mind knowing that I'm not going to forget to send a card to my Grandma on her eighty-fifth birthday. When my husband asks, "when is (enter random event) again?" I can just say "check the freaking binder dude" instead of having to rack my brain for the answer. Also, when I'm not around, everyone (including babysitters and grandparents) has quick access to all the important stuff that would otherwise just be bouncing around in my noggin.

Of course, I still get overwhelmed and my brain gets "information overload" sometimes, but once I took the time to write down my family's schedules and make those oh-so-important lists, my stress level decreased dramatically. My entire family runs so much more smoothly when everything is written down, despite our ever-increasing busy schedules.

In this chapter, I am going to include everything you will need to keep your family organized and running like a well-oiled machine. You will find calendars to help keep track of school and family schedules, contact information worksheets for friends, family, and neighbors and a perpetual calendar for birthdays and anniversaries so that you only have to write them down **one time**, instead of trying to remember them year after year.

I also wanted to give you some things that help make my daily *mom-life* easier. Every Sunday we have a "family meeting" after dinner, and it is such a fun and easy way to connect and plan the following week together as a family. I included a blank Family Meeting Agenda for you to try! It's like a little business meeting for our family and it has been something that the whole family looks forward to.

You will also find a babysitter information sheet in this chapter, which will give both the babysitter and you peace of mind on those much-needed "kid-free" nights. And speaking of kids, you are going to find a "chore list" in this chapter that is just for them! Even children as young as two years old can start helping out around the home with some small and easy chores. Picking up their toys, dusting, and helping to sort or fold laundry are jobs that even tiny toddler can do!

Remember, all of the worksheets in this book are yours as a free download! So, go ahead and write on these and see which ones work for you and your family. You can always download extra copies at any time! You can also photocopy the pages from this book and use them to create your own "family planner" just like mine.

If you take just a few minutes to fill out these pages today, not only will you immediately be more organized, but by freeing up some space in your mind, you are going to feel less stressed and much happier too.

≫

START DECLUTTERING THAT BEAUTIFUL BRAIN OF YOURS RIGHT NOW!

≪

≧ Family Schedule ≦

TIME				
6:00 A.M.				
7:00 A.M.				
8:00 A.M.				
9:00 A.M.				
10:00 A.M.				
11:00 A.M.				
12:00 P.M.				
1:00 P.M.				
2:00 P.M.				
3:00 P.M.				
4:00 P.M.				
5:00 P.M.				
6:00 P.M.				
7:00 P.M.				
8:00 P.M.				
9:00 P.M.				
10:00 P.M.				

NOTES: _____

_____

_____

≋ Family Wellness ≋

APPTS.	DOCTOR	DENTAL	EYECARE			
JANUARY						
FEBRUARY						
MARCH						
APRIL						
MAY						
JUNE						
JULY						
AUGUST						
SEPTEMBER						
OCTOBER						
NOVEMBER						
DECEMBER						

NOTES: _____

_____

_____

Perpetual Birthdays and Special Dates

JANUARY
_____
_____
_____
_____
_____
_____
_____

FEBRUARY
_____
_____
_____
_____
_____
_____
_____

MARCH
_____
_____
_____
_____
_____
_____
_____

APRIL
_____
_____
_____
_____
_____
_____
_____

MAY
_____
_____
_____
_____
_____
_____
_____

JUNE
_____
_____
_____
_____
_____
_____
_____

JULY
_____
_____
_____
_____
_____
_____
_____

AUGUST
_____
_____
_____
_____
_____
_____
_____

SEPTEMBER
_____
_____
_____
_____
_____
_____
_____

OCTOBER
_____
_____
_____
_____
_____
_____
_____

NOVEMBER
_____
_____
_____
_____
_____
_____
_____

DECEMBER
_____
_____
_____
_____
_____
_____
_____

♥ School Schedule ♥

NAME: _____

IMPORTANT DATES	ASSIGNMENT	GRADE	NOTES
/			
/			
/			
/			
/			
/			
/			
/			
/			
/			
/			
/			
/			
/			
/			
/			
/			
/			
/			
/			
/			
/			
/			
/			
/			

⩾ School Information ⩽

Child's Name: _____ Grade: _____ Bus: _____

School's Name: _____ Phone: _____

School's Address: _____

Website: _____ Login info: _____

Teacher: _____ Subject: _____ Room: ____

Email: _____ Other: _____

Teacher: _____ Subject: _____ Room: ____

Email: _____ Other: _____

Teacher: _____ Subject: _____ Room: ____

Email: _____ Other: _____

Teacher: _____ Subject: _____ Room: ____

Email: _____ Other: _____

Teacher: _____ Subject: _____ Room: ____

Email: _____ Other: _____

Child's Name: _____ Grade: _____ Bus: _____

School's Name: _____ Phone: _____

School's Address: _____

Website: _____ Login info: _____

Teacher: _____ Subject: _____ Room: ____

Email: _____ Other: _____

Teacher: _____ Subject: _____ Room: ____

Email: _____ Other: _____

Teacher: _____ Subject: _____ Room: ____

Email: _____ Other: _____

Teacher: _____ Subject: _____ Room: ____

Email: _____ Other: _____

Teacher: _____ Subject: _____ Room: ____

Email: _____ Other: _____

Your Kid's Friends
Contact Information

Friend's Name:
_____

Number: _____
Birthday: _____
Allergies/Other: _____

_____
_____

Mom's name: _____
Mom's cell: _____
Dad's name: _____
Dad's cell: _____

Friend's Name:
_____

Number: _____
Birthday: _____
Allergies/Other: _____

_____
_____

Mom's name: _____
Mom's cell: _____
Dad's name: _____
Dad's cell: _____

Friend's Name:
_____

Number: _____
Birthday: _____
Allergies/Other: _____

_____
_____

Mom's name: _____
Mom's cell: _____
Dad's name: _____
Dad's cell: _____

Friend's Name:
_____

Number: _____
Birthday: _____
Allergies/Other: _____

_____
_____

Mom's name: _____
Mom's cell: _____
Dad's name: _____
Dad's cell: _____

Friends and Family

Name: _____
Address: _____
_____
Phone: _____
Email: _____
Birthday: _____
Website: _____
Other: _____

Name: _____
Address: _____
_____
Phone: _____
Email: _____
Birthday: _____
Website: _____
Other: _____

Name: _____
Address: _____
_____
Phone: _____
Email: _____
Birthday: _____
Website: _____
Other: _____

Name: _____
Address: _____
_____
Phone: _____
Email: _____
Birthday: _____
Website: _____
Other: _____

Name: _____
Address: _____
_____
Phone: _____
Email: _____
Birthday: _____
Website: _____
Other: _____

Name: _____
Address: _____
_____
Phone: _____
Email: _____
Birthday: _____
Website: _____
Other: _____

Neighborhood Contact Information

Neighbor's Name: _____
_____
Address: _____
_____
Phone: _____
Cell: _____
Email: _____

Neighbor's Name: _____
_____
Address: _____
_____
Phone: _____
Cell: _____
Email: _____

Neighbor's Name: _____
_____
Address: _____
_____
Phone: _____
Cell: _____
Email: _____

Neighbor's Name: _____
_____
Address: _____
_____
Phone: _____
Cell: _____
Email: _____

Neighbor's Name: _____
_____
Address: _____
_____
Phone: _____
Cell: _____
Email: _____

Neighbor's Name: _____
_____
Address: _____
_____
Phone: _____
Cell: _____
Email: _____

Babysitter Information

EMERGENCY INFO
CALL 911

Parent's Name: _____

Where will we be: _____

_____

Cell phone: _____

Emergency contact: _____

Child Name: _____

Age: _____   Allergies: _____

_____

Child Name: _____

Age: _____   Allergies: _____

_____

Child Name: _____

Age: _____   Allergies: _____

_____

Child Name: _____

Age: _____   Allergies: _____

_____

NOTES:

HOUSEHOLD RULES: _____

_____

_____

_____

_____

Kid's Information

KID

Name: _____

Age: _____

Birthday: _____

Updated: _____

BEDTIME ROUTINE

_____

_____

_____

_____

_____

FOOD PREFERENCES

_____

_____

_____

_____

_____

FAVORITES

Breakfast: _____

_____

Lunch: _____

_____

Dinner: _____

_____

Snacks: _____

_____

Drink: _____

_____

Movie: _____

TV Show: _____

Music: _____

Activity: _____

Friend: _____

DAILY SCHEDULE

Wakeup: _____

Nap: _____

Bedtime: _____

Snack Time: _____

MISCELLANEOUS NOTES
(Likes, Dislikes, Fears, Etc.)

_____

_____

_____

_____

_____

_____

❧❧❧ Family Meeting Agenda ❧❧❧

WHAT'S GOING ON THIS WEEK?

_____
_____
_____
_____
_____

IDEAS FOR FAMILY FUN NIGHT:

_____
_____
_____
_____
_____

MEAL PLANNING: EVERYONE PICK A MEAL!

_____
_____
_____
_____
_____

OPEN DISCUSSION:

_____
_____
_____
_____
_____

A Journey
OF A THOUSAND MILES

BEGINS WITH A
Single Step

≋ Chapter Four ≋

ORGANIZING YOUR HOME

HOW TO GET YOUR HOME CLEAN & CLUTTER-FREE.

I can tell you first hand of the amazing and life-changing impact having a clean and organized home can have on you and your family. I lived in chaos and clutter for years and I was so accustomed to it, I didn't even realize the negative effects it was having on my mood. Stress, anxiety, and bouts of mild depression were as normal to me as the piles of junk on my bedroom floor. I never saw the correlation until the mess and clutter were finally gone for good.

I wasn't born with the organizing gene. While some people just seem to be naturally clean and tidy, my natural tendencies are that of a super slob. I leave dirty clothes on the bathroom floor and I can destroy the entire kitchen just by making a sandwich. I'm messy, always have been, and always will be. Let me assure you though, you *can* be a naturally messy person and still have a clean and organized home.

I'm a Unicorn
(In Training)

I like to call people who were born with the clean and organized gene "unicorns." You know the ones I'm talking about, those people who actually enjoy ironing their clothes, fold their underwear and arrange their bookshelves in alphabetical order. They are total "unicorns" because they are super rare and magical creatures. I can't help but be a tad jealous. I want to be a unicorn, but for now, I'll settle for being a "unicorn-in-training."

So, how can even the messiest, most disorganized person become a magical, organized unicorn-in-training? It starts with some good old-fashioned routines. A simple daily cleaning routine can really be the difference between a messy and a tidy home. Having good routines will not only make your home neat and clean, but they can also help you cut your actual cleaning time in half. A cleaner home in half the time? Yes, it is possible.

Before we dive into how a simple routine will transform your home, I want to address a misconception that so many people have about cleaning their house. I can't tell you how many clients, friends, and family (and even myself) procrastinate housework because we overestimate the amount of time it takes to actually complete a task. Do you know how long it really takes to empty the dishwasher? Wash the floor? Put away a load of laundry? The answer is: surprisingly less time that you think. The first time I actually "timed" myself emptying the dishwasher, I was completely shocked. I had always put off this simple task in the mornings because I overestimated how long it was going to take me. In reality, it takes me less than two minutes to empty the dishwasher. Two minutes!

During a recent conversation with my sister, she gasped when I told her that I mopped my kitchen every day, sometimes twice a day. She exclaimed, "I would never have time for that." When I told her it takes me just a few minutes to mop my kitchen, she insisted that it takes her a full half an hour to mop hers. Her sticky floors bothered her, but as a busy mom to three little ones, she felt like she didn't have that much extra time to dedicate to mopping. I knew exactly how she felt. I used to get so overwhelmed by the idea of how much housework I had to do and how long it would take me, that I rarely did any at all! When I jumped up, set the timer on her stove and mopped her kitchen floor, she was blown away that it took just under three minutes to wash the entire thing.

This is way more common that you think. Almost everyone overestimates how long it really takes to clean a house. I really recommend timing yourself the next time you do a household chore (like putting away a load of laundry) because it can completely change your perspective on housework and make it seem way less overwhelming.

The truth is, we often get distracted when cleaning the house. This is because we are usually forced to pick up and tidy before we can actually begin cleaning, which is the really time-consuming part.

In this book, you are going to find my daily, weekly, and spring cleaning routines along with some blank worksheets that you can design and tailor to fit your needs. I want you to give these routines a try, even if just for a week, to really see the impact they can have on your home and mood.

A CLEAN HOME IS A HAPPY HOME.

I'm not going to pretend that cleaning your house is going to solve all your problems, but it really *will* make you happier. Just by spending a few minutes to care for your home and your belongings, you will feel an immediate sense of pride and accomplishment. The one thing you can do that will have the biggest impact on your home and mood? Declutter. A big purge can immediately transform your home from messy and chaotic to clean and calm in no time flat. I can also promise you that if you let go of the unused clutter in your home, you will also be letting go of a lot of subconscious stress and anxiety you may be feeling too. I define clutter as the "excess" stuff in our homes that we don't use, don't love and just don't have the proper space for. Clutter also steals away an obnoxious amount of your precious free time. Think about all the time you've wasted looking for lost items, tidying-up messes, and dusting crap you don't even like. It's time to say, "enough is enough" and let go of the things that just are not making our lives happier or easier.

>>>

YOUR PHYSICAL SPACE HAS AN IMPACT ON YOUR EMOTIONAL WELL-BEING. MESSY, CLUTTERED SPACES MAKE US FEEL STRESSED AND SAD, WHILE CLEAN AND CLUTTER-FREE SPACES MAKE US FEEL CALM AND HAPPY.

<<<

Let's be honest, when your kitchen is cluttered and messy, not only is it depressing, but it makes preparing meals much more difficult. When your bedroom is a disaster, a mess is the first thing that greets you when you wake up in the morning and the last thing you see before you fall asleep. A messy room also makes getting ready in the morning take so much longer than it needs to.

>>>

THE MOST TELLING EXAMPLE OF HOW YOUR MESSY HOME AFFECTS YOUR MOOD, SELF-CONFIDENCE, AND WELL-BEING IS THAT FEELING YOU GET WHEN THE DOOR BELL RINGS AND YOU WERE NOT EXPECTING GUESTS.

<<<

If having unexpected guests over makes you feel ashamed of yourself, the truth is, you probably already feel that way deep down inside, even without the visitors. If you have a bad case of C.H.A.O.S. (CAN'T HAVE ANYONE OVER SYNDROME), let's cure it, once and for all, with this book!

Step one is starting with a quick and easy daily cleaning routine. I have included a simple "Busy Family Daily Cleaning Routine" that even working parents with boat loads of children can accomplish. This isn't about spending hours cleaning your home every day or making everything spotless; this is about quick daily maintenance. Even if your home is really cluttered, it's important to get into the habit of doing regular daily cleaning. **This is about taking just a few minutes every day to wipe the kitchen and bathroom counters and mop up spills on the floor each night.** It may seem like a silly thing to do when the rest of your home is drowning in clutter, but this is about developing a life long routine that will help you get the rest of your home under control.

>>>

DAILY CLEANING ROUTINES ARE ABOUT SAVING YOU TIME AND EFFORT WHEN IT COMES TO HOUSEWORK.

<<<

On top of your quick daily clean, you still have to do the regular old housework as well (groan, I know). The difference is, cleaning the house will take you way less time and effort if you have committed to basic surface cleaning each and every day.

So, what's the best method or routine for cleaning your entire home? There isn't one! Everyone is different and their cleaning styles and routines have to reflect their unique home and family. "Weekend Warriors" schedule a few hours on the weekends to clean their home from top to bottom! "Daily Speed Cleaners" do a little bit of housework throughout the day each and every day. "Zone Cleaners" prefer to clean by room or "zone" and schedule a different area for each day of the week. "Task Masters" schedule their housework based on different cleaning jobs and the tools required to complete them.

Which cleaning style best fits you and your home?

What's Your Cleaning Style?

MAKE YOUR CLEANING ROUTINE FIT YOU AND YOUR UNIQUE HOME

Discover your cleaning style by finding out what your natural habits are. Then find the right tools that work best with your cleaning style.

WEEKEND WARRIOR
Completes all housework in one day, once or twice per week.

DAILY SPEED CLEANER
Speed cleans entire home sporadically throughout the day or does one Power Hour clean per day.

ZONE CLEANERS
Cleans one room or area per day. Example: Monday-Kitchen, Tuesday-Bathrooms.

TASK MASTERS
Completes one large cleaning task per day. Example: Mondays-Dusting, Tuesday-Vacuuming.

I have included a few different types of cleaning routines in this chapter for you to test out. Give each one a try and see if you prefer zone cleaning or perhaps daily speed cleaning. For me, I use a daily Dirty Thirty cleaning routine combined with a more in depth weekly task master cleaning schedule squeezed in here and there. **The great thing is that you can really make your cleaning routine fit you and your unique home.** You can tailor your routine to fit your schedule and your personality. There is no wrong way to clean, the important thing is that you incorporate a cleaning routine into your schedule, no matter which style you choose.

Once you have made regular house cleaning part of your daily or weekly routine, the next step for transforming your home is to kick the clutter to the curb.

My absolute favorite part of this entire chapter is the Decluttering Guide. For me, decluttering has had the biggest and most profound impact on my home and my life. So many people are moving towards a simpler and more minimal lifestyle—and for good reason. Having less "stuff" means having less stress, spending less time cleaning, less time looking for lost items, and having MORE money and time for you and your family. I had no idea how negatively my clutter was affecting me, until I finally got rid of the excess junk. I literally removed truckload after truckload of unused items from my home over the course of a year. The result? I was happier, I was healthier, and I was finally able to fall in LOVE with my home.

Decluttering is the fastest and easiest way to improve the look, function, and feel of your home. Not only is purging your excess stuff free, but it can also MAKE you money in the process! I have had real success selling my gently used items on Facebook swap sites. With these local online yard sale groups, you can sell your items faster and for more money than a traditional yard sale, and you can do it all from your smart phone!

While I do recommend selling the more expensive items that you are no longer using or loving, there is something to be said for just giving your clutter away to charity (or even...gasp...the garbage can). Sometimes, trying to sell your used items can be time-consuming and tedious. It can also delay your progress and get in the way of your momentum. When I was going through my "purging process" in the beginning, I quickly realized that while the extra money was wonderful, what I really needed was more time and less work in my life. I found a local charity, which would come to my home and pick up my donations, right from my front door! **Simplifying your life means just that; doing things the simple way.** Give yourself grace and just let go of the pressures to have everything the "right" or "best" way and focus on just getting the important stuff done. Having less in life is about more than just our physical items, it's about letting go of the guilt and negative feelings that come along with our clutter.

So, start your decluttering challenge today. Letting go of unloved stuff is a critical part of having an organized home, but it doesn't have to be an overwhelming and monumental undertaking. You can have a clean and clutter-free home in just fifteen-minute intervals, and this Decluttering Guide can help you get started. **Commit to doing the easy challenges in this chapter and kick your clutter to the curb, without the stress or mess of traditional decluttering methods.** In this guide, I will walk you through the process of purging your home, step-by-step and room by room, so you can have a clutter-free home in as little as fifteen minutes a day.

Once you have decluttered your home, it's time to get organized! The most effective way to organize any space is by utilizing the S.P.A.C.E. technique. I break down this organizing method in my first book, *Real Life Organizing*, but as it is such a critical part of getting your home organized, I created a "S.P.A.C.E. CHALLENGE" in this chapter as a helpful guide. This method is fail proof and makes organizing any space really simple and straightforward. I learned this method from the amazing and talented Julie Morgenstern in her must-read book *Organizing from the Inside Out* and I was finally able to stop just rearranging my stuff, and instead create "a home for everything and have everything in its home."

My go-to organizing system has been, and always will be, dollar store containers! Once you follow the steps outlined in the S.P.A.C.E Challenge, you will see that "contain" is one of those important steps. Finding containers for your belongings doesn't have to be expensive and it can even be free. So many of my followers have shared photos of their homes organized with recycled boxes and empty food containers and they have made their homes beautifully organized without spending a dime. Pinterest is bursting with amazingly inexpensive and even free organizing solutions for your entire home. I don't want you to ever be discouraged from organizing based on time or money restrictions. Organization is about making your life easier and your home more functional, not about having some magazine-worthy space.

Getting organized also isn't going to happen overnight. It's a process, but it can actually be really fun and rewarding. The secret to loving organization and not getting in over your head is to just do one small area at a time. Maybe today you can take five minutes to organize your sock drawer and tomorrow you make a home for all your extra light bulbs. Creating a "home" inside your home for all of your belongings is exactly what organization is all about.

> "A PLACE FOR EVERYTHING AND EVERYTHING IN ITS PLACE."
> —BENJAMIN FRANKLIN

The real secret to *keeping* your home organized for the long term is regular clutter maintenance. Unfortunately, organizing isn't a "one and done" type thing. Just as we are constantly bringing new things into our homes, we need to make sure we are taking out the old stuff at the same pace. I can't tell you how many times I organized areas in my home, just to have them messy again a few weeks later. For a perpetually clutter-free home, you have to make purging part of your regular routine. I suggest making an easy and effective **21-Item Toss** part of your weekly or monthly cleaning routine. A 21-Item Toss is a purging technique where you grab a bag or box and find twenty-one items in your home to toss, donate, or recycle as quickly as possible. **The magic number twenty-one is just high enough to push yourself, but low enough to reach in just a few minutes of purging without being overwhelming**. In this chapter, I have included twenty-one examples of items that you can easily purge from your home today!

>>>

MAKE PURGING PART OF YOUR REGULAR ROUTINE—IT'S WHAT IS GOING TO KEEP YOUR HOME CLUTTER-FREE FOR GOOD.

<<<

The other amazing benefit to regular cleaning and organizing is that it can really help you fall in love with your home. I often suffer from a bad case of house envy. Sometimes after visiting friends in their new, beautiful homes or after seeing breathtaking spaces on Pinterest or Instagram, I feel a little bad about my own small and dated house. It's during these times that I give my home a "hug" by tidying-up a space or organizing a drawer. I instantly feel a little more love, respect and appreciation for what I have when I've taken a second to care for it.

Remember, it doesn't matter what your décor looks like or what size your house is; a clean home is a beautiful one. By making your quick daily cleaning routines a priority, you are ensuring that your home is always the relaxing and beautiful oasis that you and your family deserve.

Speaking of family! Don't forget to get your children involved! I have included my "Summer Chore Kit" so that you can create easy chore kits for your children to use. It's an easy and effective way to teach children how to properly clean, and take some of the work away from you. Simply load up three containers with various cleaning supplies and attach the cleaning checklists to the front of those containers for a simple and straight forward cleaning kit for kids.

Want to make sure that the supplies you and your family use are natural and chemical free? Try my **Homemade Cleaning Supplies** recipes! Add your favorite essential oils for a little extra aromatherapy while you make your home sparkle.

So, let's get started on your journey to the home of your dreams. It is much easier and much less work than you think! Little by little, step-by-step, you are going to fall in love with your home a make it the oasis you deserve.

≫

DON'T CLEAN YOUR HOME BECAUSE YOU HAVE TO. DO IT BECAUSE YOU DESERVE IT.

≪

✿Daily Cleaning Checklist✿

MORNING

- ○ Make Beds
- ○ Empty Dishwasher
- ○ Clean Kitchen
- ○ Wipe Bathrooms
- ○ Plan Day
- ○ _____
- ○ _____
- ○ _____
- ○ _____

CHOOSE ONE OR TWO

- ○ Dust House
- ○ Mop House
- ○ Vacuum House
- ○ Clean Bathrooms
- ○ Clean Bedrooms
- ○ Deep Clean Kitchen
- ○ Declutter
- ○ Wash Bedding
- ○ _____
- ○ _____
- ○ _____
- ○ _____

EVENING

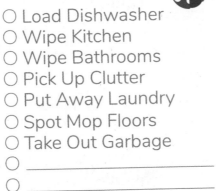

- ○ Load Dishwasher
- ○ Wipe Kitchen
- ○ Wipe Bathrooms
- ○ Pick Up Clutter
- ○ Put Away Laundry
- ○ Spot Mop Floors
- ○ Take Out Garbage
- ○ _____
- ○ _____
- ○ _____
- ○ _____

DO ONCE A MONTH

- ○ Windows
- ○ Light Fixtures
- ○ Baseboards
- ○ Appliances
- ○ Picture Frames
- ○ _____
- ○ _____
- ○ _____
- ○ _____

Cleaning Schedule

DAILY

- [ ] _____
- [ ] _____
- [ ] _____
- [ ] _____
- [ ] _____
- [ ] _____
- [ ] _____
- [ ] _____
- [ ] _____

MONDAY

- [ ] _____
- [ ] _____
- [ ] _____

TUESDAY

- [ ] _____
- [ ] _____
- [ ] _____

WEDNESDAY

- [ ] _____
- [ ] _____
- [ ] _____

THURSDAY

- [ ] _____
- [ ] _____
- [ ] _____

FRIDAY

- [ ] _____
- [ ] _____
- [ ] _____

SATURDAY

- [ ] _____
- [ ] _____
- [ ] _____

SUNDAY

- [ ] _____
- [ ] _____
- [ ] _____

Chore List for the Busy Family

MORNING

- [ ] Make Beds
- [ ] Empty Dishwasher
- [ ] Reload Dishwasher
- [ ] Put in a Load of Laundry
- [ ] Wipe Bathroom Counters
- [ ] _____
- [ ] _____
- [ ] _____
- [ ] _____

15-MINUTE BLOCKS OF TIME

Take about 15-minute blocks throughout your day to accomplish your chores.

AFTERNOON

- [ ] Make Dinner
- [ ] Help Kids with Homework/Crafts
- [ ] Organize a Drawer
- [ ] Switch over Laundry
- [ ] _____
- [ ] _____
- [ ] _____
- [ ] _____
- [ ] _____

BEFORE BED

- [ ] Clean Kitchen Counter & Sink
- [ ] Put Away Laundry
- [ ] Spot Mop Floors
- [ ] Wipe Down Bathroom
- [ ] Run Dishwasher
- [ ] Wipe Down Tables, Surfaces, & Mirrors in Main Living Areas
- [ ] _____
- [ ] _____

WEEKLY TO-DO

- [ ] Vacuum House Very Well
- [ ] Dust Home
- [ ] Empty Garbage
- [ ] Pay Bills
- [ ] Clean Out Fridge
- [ ] Scrub Bathrooms
- [ ] Wash Floors
- [ ] 21-Item Toss
- [ ] _____
- [ ] _____
- [ ] _____
- [ ] _____

Dirty 30 Speed Cleaning List

LET'S TAKE 30 MINUTES TO CLEAN AS FAST AS WE CAN

READY? SET. CLEAN!

- ○ Make Beds
- ○ Do Dishes
- ○ Clean Kitchen
- ○ Clean Bathroom
- ○ Tidy Tote Pick Up
- ○ Clean Surfaces
- ○ Spot Mop
- ○ Laundry
- ○ _____
- ○ _____
- ○ _____
- ○ _____

It's not about deep cleaning.
This is about having a clean &
tidy home as fast as possible.

Weekly Speed Cleaning Schedule

FOR 15 MINUTES A DAY

Follow this cleaning schedule for a home that looks professionally cleaned! Use this list and your 15-Minute Nightly Cleaning Routine for a perfectly clutter-free and clean home!

MONDAY

- ☑ Dust All Flat Surfaces
- ☐ _____
- ☐ _____
- ☐ _____

TUESDAY

- ☑ Vacuum All the Floors
- ☐ _____
- ☐ _____
- ☐ _____

WEDNESDAY

- ☑ Mop All the Floors
- ☐ _____
- ☐ _____
- ☐ _____

THURSDAY

- ☑ Spot Clean Messy Areas
- ☐ _____
- ☐ _____
- ☐ _____

FRIDAY

- ☑ Wipe Kitchen Cupboards & Appliances
- ☐ _____
- ☐ _____

SATURDAY

- ☑ Scrub Bathrooms
- ☐ _____
- ☐ _____
- ☐ _____

SUNDAY

- ☑ Family Tidy Time. Declutter for 15 Minutes.
- ☐ _____
- ☐ _____

READY? GET SET. GO!!!

Weekly Zone Cleaning Routine

MONDAY

BATHROOMS
- ○ Clean Mirrors
- ○ Clean Toilet
- ○ Clean Sinks & Counters
- ○ Clean Tubs/Showers
- ○ Clean Floors & Baseboards
- ○ Replace Towels & Bathmats

TUESDAY

LIVING ROOMS
- ○ Declutter & Straighten
- ○ Dust Shelves, Blinds & TV
- ○ Vacuum / Sweep
- ○ Clean Glass / Windows
- ○ Wipe Remotes
- ○ Dust Artwork / Pictures

WEDNESDAY

KITCHEN
- ○ Deep Clean Counter tops
- ○ Wipe Down Appliances
- ○ Wipe Down Stove Top
- ○ Clean Microwave
- ○ Wipe Down Cabinets
- ○ Vacuum / Sweep Floors

THURSDAY

DINING ROOM & ENTRY
- ○ Declutter & Straighten
- ○ Dust Surfaces
- ○ Wipe Down Windows
- ○ Tidy & Put Away Misc. Items
- ○ Vacuum / Sweep
- ○ Tackle One Bi-monthly Task

FRIDAY

BEDROOM
- ○ Declutter & Straighten
- ○ Dust Surfaces & Blinds
- ○ Change Bed Sheets
- ○ Pick Up Clothes
- ○ Vacuum / Sweep
- ○ Wipe Artwork / Pictures

WEEKEND

OUTSIDE & GARAGE
- ○ Clean Deep Freezer / Fridge
- ○ Wipe Outdoor Furniture
- ○ Declutter Garage
- ○ Sweep / Rake / Mow
- ○ Weed Garden / Yard
- ○ Tackle One Monthly Task

Choose a day in each month to complete a yearly cleaning task.

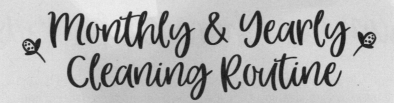

Monthly & Yearly Cleaning Routine

MONTHLY

- ○ Deep Clean Windows
- ○ Wash Car
- ○ Declutter Garage
- ○ Tidy Pantry
- ○ Vacuum Couch Cushions
- ○ Declutter a Closet
- ○ _____
- ○ _____
- ○ _____
- ○ _____

BI-MONTHLY

- ○ Clean Microwave
- ○ Clean Stove top/Oven
- ○ Clean Dishwasher
- ○ Clean Out Fridge/Freezer
- ○ Clean Washer & Dryer
- ○ Clean Trash Cans
- ○ Clean Toasters
- ○ Clean Baseboards
- ○ Clean Cabinets
- ○ Wipe Handrails
- ○ _____
- ○ _____
- ○ _____
- ○ _____

Add one or two of these monthly, bi-monthly, and yearly cleaning routines to your weekly schedule.

YEARLY

JAN-MAR

- ○ Change Filters
- ○ Organize Personal Files
- ○ Prepare Tax Information
- ○ Change Batteries for Smoke Detectors
- ○ _____
- ○ _____

APR-JUN

- ○ Purge Items in Kitchen
- ○ Clean Curtains
- ○ Toss Expired Medicines
- ○ Purge Towel Cabinet
- ○ _____
- ○ _____

JUL-SEP

- ○ Purge Clothing
- ○ Defrost Freezer
- ○ Deep Clean Carpets/Rugs
- ○ Refresh Decorative Pillows
- ○ _____
- ○ _____

OCT-DEC

- ○ Purge Holiday Decorations
- ○ Purge Kid Toys
- ○ Purge Bathroom Products
- ○ Clean Garage
- ○ _____
- ○ _____

❧ Summer Chore Kit for Kids ❧

Print, cut, and attach these cleaning checklists to the front of a baskets.
Fill baskets with cleaning supplies (label cleaners for smaller children).

KID'S CHORE KIT
BATHROOM

- ☐ Spray Shower
- ☐ Spray Inside Toilet
- ☐ Pick Up Towels/Clothes
- ☐ Spot Clean Mirrors
- ☐ Spray & Wipe Counter
- ☐ Wipe Toilet
- ☐ Mop Floors

KID'S CHORE KIT
DUSTING

- ☐ Pick One Room
- ☐ Put Away Clutter
- ☐ Use Duster for High Places
- ☐ Move Items Off Tables
- ☐ Spray & Wipe Tables
- ☐ Put Items Back
- ☐ Straighten Pillows

KID'S CHORE KIT
KITCHEN

- ☐ Empty/Load Dishwasher
- ☐ Put Away Clutter
- ☐ Spray & Wipe Counters
- ☐ Spray & Wipe Appliances
- ☐ Wipe Cabinet Fronts
- ☐ Spot Sweep Floors
- ☐ Mop Kitchen

SCREEN CHECKLIST
NO SCREEN TIME UNTIL:

- ☐ Bed is Made
- ☐ Room is Clean
- ☐ Eat Breakfast
- ☐ Get Dressed
- ☐ Brush Teeth & Hair
- ☐ 20 Minutes of Chores
- ☐ 20 Minutes Outside

Spring Cleaning Checklist from Top to Bottom

TOP

STEP 1

☐ Declutter and Dishes

STEP 2

☐ Dust Kitchen Cabinets
☐ Wash Blinds
☐ Clean Light Fixtures
☐ Remove Cobwebs
☐ Dust Doors & Windows
☐ Clean Front Door

☐ Check Smoke Alarms
☐ Dust Ceiling Vents
☐ Dust Pictures & Art
☐ Clean Top of Fridge
☐ Wash Windows
☐ Vacuum Curtains

STEP 3

☐ Flip Mattress
☐ Scrub Shower & Tub
☐ Clean Out Freezer
☐ Vacuum Upholstered Furniture

☐ Deep Clean Oven
☐ Change Furnace Filter
☐ Dust Flat Surfaces
☐ Wipe Out Kitchen Cabinets & Drawers

STEP 4

☐ Clean Under Furniture
☐ Dust Baseboard
☐ Clean Under Beds
☐ Clean Behind Fridge
☐ Clean Behind Stove
☐ Check Dryer Vent Hose
☐ Clean Under Beds
☐ Clean Bottom of All Toilets
☐ Scrub/Reseal Tile, Grout, Caulking in Bathrooms & Kitchen If Needed

☐ Wash Bed Skirts
☐ Vacuum Bottom of Closets
☐ Sweep Garage
☐ Dust Clean Air Returns
☐ Mop Floors
☐ Clean Garbage Cans
☐ Spot Clean Carpet Stains
☐ Wash Kick Plate in Kitchen
☐ Wipe Out Cabinets Under All Sinks

BOTTOM

❧Home Maintenance Log❧

FREQUENCY	MAINTENANCE TASK	COST	DATE COMPLETED PER SEASON			

CLUTTERBUG

15-MINUTE
HOME DECLUTTERING
GUIDE

Having a clean and organized home always begins with purging! Join me for "The Great Purge of 2018" as we kick the clutter to the curb and finally get organized for good. So let's get started. We are going to declutter our homes, room by room, in just 15 minutes a day!

MASTER BEDROOM

READY? GET SET, GO!
Set your timer and see how many things you can get done!

DONE	TASK TO TACKLE
	CLEAR OFF THE TOP OF DRESSER. Put away things that belong in your bedroom. Toss the garbage and donate anything you no longer need. If anything does not belong in your bedroom, simply set in "Does Not Belong" bin and leave it there until the entire room has been decluttered.
	LET IT GO! Donate 21 items from your dresser drawers. Find at least 6 pairs of old socks and 4 pairs of underwear that can go!
	FLOOR TIME! Pick up clothing and anything that is laying on your floor. Move fast! Put things away, use your donate and DNB bin as well as your trash bags until the floor is clean.
	CLOSET CHALLENGE! Purge and donate 21 items from your closet right now! Remember the 80/20 rule: you wear only 20% of your clothing 80% of the time. If you wouldn't buy it again, it's time to let it go.
	HANG IT UP! Take a few minutes and turn all of the hangers in your closet backwards. Put the hangers back normally as you wear the clothing and put it away next time. In six months or so, anything still backwards should be donated...you never wear it!
	MONSTERS UNDER THE BED! Let's check for those monsters under the bed! Anything you can let go into the donate bin or trash? Find at least 5 things from under there!
	CLUTTER HOT SPOTS! Clutter Hot Spots - night tables, hooks, chairs, TV stand. Move quickly and declutter these areas. Try and find 10 items from these cluttered areas that you can get rid of now!

YOU'VE PURGED OVER 65 THINGS FROM YOUR BEDROOM!

≋CONGRATULATIONS≋

 **CLUTTERBUG**

✦ KITCHEN ✦

DONE	TASK TO TACKLE
	LOSE THE LIDS.
	Say goodbye to those extra lids we all have in our food storage container area. While you're are at it, find 3 unused containers to donate.
	SEE YA SPATULAS!
	Purge 2 extra-large serving spoons, spatulas, or that extra potato masher you never use.
	SMALL APPLIANCES.
	Donate 1 small appliance that you never, ever use. Here are some examples: rice cooker, bread maker, food processor, hand blender, or toaster oven. If they haven't been used in 6 months, it's time to let them go.
	MIS-MATCHED MUGS HAVE GOT TO GO!
	Really, how often do you have 20 friends over for coffee at the exact same time? There is no need to have so many mugs. Let 4 ugly ones go!
	THE HORRORS UNDER THE SINK.
	Take a minute and purge some unused cleaners, grocery bags, and those dust-collecting vases from under your kitchen sink. Get rid of at least 5 things right now!
	PURGE THE PANTRY.
	Go through your pantry and donate 5 food items that you will never eat. Your local food bank will appreciate your kindness and your pantry will appreciate the newfound space! Don't forget to toss all expired items.
	DON'T FORGET THE FREEZER!
	Meat is expensive, but you are never going to eat that freezer-burnt chicken so let it go. Find 5 things from your freezer to toss today.
	YOU ARE ALMOST DONE.
	Find 5 other random things to purge from your kitchen today. Here are some examples: duplicate measuring spoons, scratched pots and pans, chipped glasses and plates, and worn-out baking pans.
	PUT THE JUNK IN YOUR TRUNK.
	Find 5 things from your junk drawer that can be tossed or donated.

≋CONGRATULATIONS≋

YOU'VE PURGED OVER 35 THINGS FROM YOUR KITCHEN!

➤LIVING AREA◄

DONE	TASK TO TACKLE
	KNICK-KNACKS ARE NICE, BUT ONLY IN MODERATION. Go through your home and find five home decor accessories or knick-knacks that you no longer love and can let go to someone else.
	BYE-BYE BOOKS. You really CAN have too many. Try and find 10 books that you will never read again and share your love of reading.
	MANAGE YOUR MAGAZINES. I love buying magazines at the checkout stand, but once I've read them, they instantly turn into clutter! Purge 10 old magazines (or newspapers or flyers) today.
	DVD CASE CLUTTER. The best way to organize your DVD collection is to let go of the cases and use a DVD sleeve organizer. Trust me, toss those cases. You will thank me later!
	PURGE SOME PICTURE FRAMES. I know, this one may hurt a bit, but too many picture frames is making your space look cluttered. Take the pictures out and donate 4 frames from your home right now.
	GOODBYE GAMES. I love game night, but there are plenty of board games I'm storing that we never even play. Let go of 3 board games or puzzles and pass on the fun to another family.
	TAME THE TECH. Outdated video games, extra remote controls, and unused tech devices are adding to the clutter in your home. Find 4 old pieces of technology that can be donated.
	REIGN IN THE RANDOM. Find 5 extra random things in your home, from any space, that you can let go of right now.

YOU'VE PURGED OVER 41 THINGS FROM YOUR LIVING AREA!

≥CONGRATULATIONS≤

CLUTTERBUG

➤BATHROOM➤

READY? GET SET, GO!
Set your timer and see how many
things you can get done!

DONE	TASK TO TACKLE
	BREAK UP WITH YOUR MAKEUP. If you don't love the color, it's time to let it go. Purge 10 things from your makeup collection that you never wear.
	OUT WITH THE OLD. Go through your medication and donate anything expired. Try and find 5 old medicines or first aid supplies that are past their prime.
	LET GO OF THE LOTIONS. We all have those extra lotions and face potions that we never even use. They take up valuable space in our bathrooms and need to go! Let go of the goo (at least 5 bottles)!
	TIRED-LOOKING TOWELS. Nothing is worse than getting out of a nice, hot shower and having to dry off with an old, stained towel. Find 3 towels that have seen better days and donate them to your local animal shelter.
	EMPTY OUT THE EMPTIES. We all have them! You know what I mean, those empty bottles of shampoo or toothpaste that we still haven't thrown out for some reason! Toss them now!
	PASS ON THE PRODUCTS. Maybe it's expensive perfume, or that curling iron that you really don't like. Whatever it is, find 5 unused products that you can pass onto a friend or family member today.
	TOSS THOSE TOOTHBRUSHES. Once you buy a new toothbrush, toss out the old one! I know you can find some old toothbrushes to toss in your drawer.
	CLEAN OUT THE CLEANING SUPPLIES. If you haven't used it in the past 6 months, it's time to get rid of at least 2 unused cleaning products from under your sink.

⇌CONGRATULATIONS⇌

**YOU'VE PURGED OVER 30 THINGS
FROM YOUR BATHROOM!**

CLUTTERBUG

>CLUTTER HOTSPOT<

DONE	TASK TO TACKLE
	CONTAIN THE COUNTER CLUTTER. Get a pretty basket to contain the clutter that tends to collect on your kitchen counter and find 5 things that can just go.
	PURGE THE PAPER. Take just 15 minutes to go through and shred and recycle at least 30 old paid bills, junk mail, receipts, or other paper from your home that you no longer need.
	JUNK DRAWER TIME. Find 5 things from your junk drawer that are actual junk and can be tossed right now!
	ENTICING ENTRANCE WAY. Take a few minutes to purge old shoes, purses, jackets, or other things from your entrance today. Find at least 5 things that can go.
	LOVE YOUR LAUNDRY AREA. Give your laundry area a little TLC by clearing out some clutter. Toss old cleaners you never use, lost or holey socks, broken laundry baskets, and take a few minutes to tidy up this high-use area right now.
	CLEAR OUT THE CLEANING SUPPLIES. We all have cleaning supplies that we have bought, but never use. Take a few minutes and purge 5 cleaning products that are doing nothing except contributing to the mess.
	STORAGE SPACE TIME. Say goodbye to 10 items that you have been "storing" in your home. Choose items that you have not used in the past 12 months and finally let them go! Search your garage, basement, or other storage areas and make some much-needed space for the things you actually love and use.

YOU'VE PURGED OVER 60 THINGS FROM YOUR HOME!

≷CONGRATULATIONS≷

⚘ S.P.A.C.E. ⚘
CHALLENGE

If you just completed everything in this Decluttering guide so far, you have just removed over 300 unused things from your home.

Now, let's keep this momentum going and continue organizing your home using the S.P.A.C.E. organizing method!

Pick an area of your home that you want to organize. Make sure the area is small enough that you can complete in just 15 minutes. You will find some areas to choose from on the following page. Now, let's get organized for good using this method:

S   Sort all of the items from this space into "like" piles on the floor or other flat surface. Keep your piles separated by category. Here is an example: if you are doing your bathroom closet, make a pile for "first aid supplies," "medications," "vitamins," and "personal hygiene." Keep sorting until your entire space is empty.

P   Now it's time to purge. Go through each pile and let go of old, unused, or duplicate items that you no longer want to keep. Be ruthless!

A   Let's assign a place for these newly sorted piles to call home! Which of these things do you use the most often? The items you use the most often should be the easiest to access, so place these at waist or eye level. The items you rarely use should be stored on top shelves or in harder to reach areas. You may want to consider moving items to an entirely different space in your home during this time.

C   Contain! This is my favorite part. Measure the areas that you have "assigned" as new homes for you piles and find containers that will fit that space! Be sure the containers are large enough to hold everything in your sorted pile. Get creative! Reuse containers you already have or shop your local dollar store for budget-friendly options.

E   Evaluate your newly organized space from time to time to make sure it is still working for you! Make purging a part of your regular cleaning routine so that it never becomes out of control again.

≥YOU CAN DO THIS≤

"DON'T LIMIT YOUR CHALLENGES, CHALLENGE YOUR LIMITS."

NEED MORE SPACE?

30-DAY DECLUTTERING CHALLENGE

SORT • PURGE • ASSIGN • CONTAIN • EVALUATE

Organize one area a day for 30 days using the S.P.A.C.E. Method.

SET YOUR TIMER FOR JUST 15 MINUTES EACH DAY. YOU WILL BE AMAZED AT HOW MUCH YOU CAN ACCOMPLISH IN JUST 15 MINUTES.

1. UNDER KITCHEN SINK
2. FOOD CONTAINERS
3. BAKEWARE & DISHES
4. UTENSIL DRAWERS
5. FRIDGE
6. FREEZER
7. PANTRY
8. JUNK DRAWER
9. LINEN CLOSET
10. BATHROOM DRAWERS
11. UNDER BATHROOM SINK
12. MEDICINE/TOILETRIES
13. DRESSER DRAWERS
14. UNDER YOUR BED
15. CLOSET

16. SHOES
17. PURSES, BAGS, TOTES
18. MEMORABILIA
19. CHILDREN'S TOYS
20. CHILDREN'S CLOTHES
21. CRAFT SUPPLIES
22. LAUNDRY AREA
23. DESK/PAPERWORK
24. STORAGE AREA
25. BOOKS
26. MOVIES/GAMES
27. OUTERWEAR
28. CLUTTERED SURFACES
29. GARAGE/SHED
30. TOOLS

"DON'T LIMIT YOUR CHALLENGES, CHALLENGE YOUR LIMITS."

≥YOU CAN DO THIS≤

✤Best Homemade Cleaners✤

MULTI-PURPOSE CLEANER

- 3 Cups Warm Water
- 1 Teaspoon Baking Soda
- 1 Teaspoon Borax (Optional)
- 1 Teaspoon Glycerin
  (or Dish Soap)
- 10 Drops of Essential Oil

GLASS CLEANER

- 1 Cup Hydrogen Peroxide
- 1½ Cups of Warm Water
- ½ Cups of Rubbing Alcohol
  (Isopropyl Alcohol)
- 1 Teaspoon Cornstarch
  (Secret ingredient)
- 10 Drops of Essential Oil

DISINFECTANT SPRAY

- 1 Cup Hydrogen Peroxide
- ¼ Cup Lemon Juice
- 1¾ Cups Warm Water
- 2 Drops of Dish Soap
- 10 Drops of Lavender and/or
  Tea Tree Oil

GRANITE CLEANER

- 1 Cup Rubbing Alcohol
- 2 Cups Warm Water
- 2 Drops Dish Soap
- 10 Drops Essential Oil
  (Not Citrus)

❧ Best Homemade Cleaners ❧

POWDER LAUNDRY DETERGENT

- 8 Cups of Borax
- 1 Box of Baking Soda
- 1 Container of OxiClean
  (or Generic Brand Substitute)
- 1 Bar of Soap Grated
- 40 Drops of Your Favorite
  Essential Oil

CLOTHING STAIN REMOVER

- 1 Cup Hydrogen Peroxide
- 10 Drops Dish Soap
- 5 Teaspoons of Baking Soda

Mix together to make liquid paste. Store in airtight container. Lightly rub to stain with a toothbrush. Leave for one hour before washing.

LAUNDRY PODS

- 1 Bar of Soap Grated
- 3 Cups of Borax
- 3 Cups Washing/Baking Soda
- 1 Cup of OxiClean
- 1 Cup of Vinegar

Add the vinegar slowly to mixture. Press mixture firmly into ice cube trays and let dry for 24 hours. Pop out and use.

DRYER SHEETS

- 1 Cup Fabric Softener
- 6 Cups of Water

Add ½ sponges to your mixture. Toss sponge and your laundry into your dryer for softer clothes. Place used sponges back into solution and reuse.

Twenty-One Item Toss

HERE ARE 21 EXAMPLES OF ITEMS YOU CAN PURGE!

READY? SET. PURGE!

1. Old Electronics (Phone, Ear buds, etc.)
2. Stained or Old Towels
3. Burnt-Down Candles
4. Old Nail Polish
5. T-shirts You Never Wear
6. Holey Socks
7. Worn-Out Bras
8. Expired Vitamins & Medications
9. Worn-Out Underwear
10. Old Purses
11. Faded Old Sheets
12. Empty Boxes
13. Bills & Statements Over 1-Year Old
14. Expired Coupons
15. Hair Accessories You Never Wear
16. Makeup Older than 10 Months
17. Christmas Décor You Never Put Out
18. Skin Care Products You Don't Like
19. DVDs You Don't Watch
20. Clothes That Are Too Small or Big
21. Old Newsletters, Flyers, or Other Outdated Paper

Laundry Cheat Sheet

LAUNDRY ITEM	WATER TEMP	DETERGENT	ADD	DRYER SHEET	DRYING METHOD
Baby Clothes	Hot	✓	Softener	✗	Machine Warm
Jeans	Cold	✓	Softener	✓	Machine Warm
Kitchen Towels	Warm	✓	Bleach	✓	Machine Hot
Lingerie	Cold	✓	Soda	✗	Hang
Pajamas	Hot	✓	Softener	✓	Machine Hot
Shirts	Warm	✓	Softener	✓	Machine Warm
Stained Items	Warm	✓	Soda	✗	Machine Warm
Sweaters	Cold	✓	Softener	✗	Hang
Towels	Hot	✓	Bleach	✓	Machine Hot
Whites	Hot	✓	Bleach	✓	Machine Hot

Stain Guide

INK
USE: Rubbing Alcohol

COFFEE OR TEA
USE: Vinegar

WINE
USE: Peroxide & Dish Soap

MAKEUP
USE: Rubbing Alcohol

SWEAT
USE: Peroxide & Soda

GRASS
USE: Vinegar & Cold Water

BLOOD
USE: Cold Salt Water & Peroxide

THIS HOME HAS
Endless
LOVE & LAUNDRY

≋ Chapter Five ≋

ORGANIZING YOUR MEALS

HOW TO SAVE TIME, MONEY, AND EAT HEALTHIER WITH MEAL PLANNING.

Of all the organizing systems that you can set up in your home, nothing is going to save you more time and money than meal planning. I was reluctant to meal plan for so long. Actually, it wasn't reluctance as much as forgetfulness. I had the best intentions of weekly meal planning, but I would either forget about it completely, or I wouldn't plan properly. Either way, almost every night was a frantic hustle to get dinner on the table, and I hated every minute of it. I don't love cooking at the best of times, so throwing meals together with little to no planning never ended well.

It has only been the past year that I have really rocked this meal-planning thing, and let me tell you, my family is ecstatic. While I am certainly no Martha Stewart, our family dinners have drastically improved. No more fish stuffed with stovetop stuffing (yes, I did and yes it was as gross as it sounds) or burnt chicken still frozen on the inside. Now that I have my meals planned and all the ingredients on hand, cooking has started to become less of a dreaded chore and much more enjoyable, which means I do a much better job preparing meals. I also save our family a lot of money, we eat healthier meals, and my kids stopped complaining about what I make for dinner. What's not to love about this easy organizing solution?

So, let's jump right in! To really get into the full swing of weekly meal planning, I had to change a few of my **bad meal habits** first.

Bad Meal Habit #1 – I decided what to make for dinner every night only minutes before I started cooking. This was a terrible habit because it was a total crapshoot if I had everything I needed, but worst of all, I wasn't involving my family in the dinner making decisions. Nothing is worse then slaving away cooking for your family, only to have them complain or not eat it at all. **Let everyone in the family be involved in choosing the meals for the following week.**

≫

BY INVOLVING YOUR FAMILY IN MEAL PLANNING
AND LETTING EVERYONE PICK ONE MEAL PER WEEK,
YOU MAKE DINNER TIME MUCH MORE ENJOYABLE
FOR EVERYONE.

≪

Not only will your kids enjoy the dinner that they have chosen, but they will also be more respectful of everyone else's meal choices as well. We have a "family meeting" every Sunday night, right after dinner, where we plan the meals and family activities for the following week. I really recommend having an adorable little business meeting with your family, where everyone can get involved in planning your weekly meals. You can find our "Family Meeting Agenda" in the previous chapter.

Bad Meal Habit #2 – I went grocery shopping every few days, and only bought enough food for a few meals at a time. What makes this a bad habit is, when life got busy and there wasn't time to grocery shop, we often had to resort to fast food. Not only was this unhealthy and expensive, but it also made me feel like a failure as a mom.

➤➤➤

PLANNING MEALS FOR THE ENTIRE WEEK GIVES YOU THE ABILITY TO GROCERY SHOP FOR THE ENTIRE WEEK, WHICH MEANS NO MORE LAST-MINUTE FAST FOOD.

⫷⫷

When meal planning, plan the ENTIRE WEEK at one time. Of course, you can still schedule in the occasional fast food dinner or pizza night, but when you have a full seven days of meals planned in advance, you never have to worry about having nothing for dinner. Once you have your meals planned, make your grocery-shopping list and include everything you will need for the full seven days of meals. In this chapter, you will find a grocery-shopping list that you can laminate and use over and over again with a dry erase marker to make sure you have everything you need to make delicious and healthy family meals.

Bad Meal Habit #3 – My meal plan wasn't visible. When I did take the time to plan our weekly meals, I often forgot what I had planned, which totally defeated the purpose. It's important to write your meal plan in two places. **The first is on a paper that you can bring with you to the grocery store, along with your grocery-shopping list.** This is important because it really helps you if you need to adjust your shopping list based on coupons, sales or the freshness of the meat and produce. Maybe you planned on having steak and cauliflower, but your grocery store had fresh corn on sale. It's nice to have your meal plan with you so that you know exactly what day/meal you are buying for.

The second place to keep your weekly meal plan is displayed in your kitchen on a menu board.

A MENU BOARD IS A GREAT REMINDER OF WHAT YOU NEED TO TAKE OUT FOR DINNER, BUT IT ALSO STOPS THE DREADED "WHAT'S FOR DINNER" WHINING FROM YOUR KIDS. YOU'RE WELCOME.

I like to display my menu planner in a dollar store picture frame right on my kitchen counter. Not only is this pretty, but it is a really functional part of my kitchen décor. Go ahead and cut the menu planner from this book and place it in a frame! You can use a dry erase marker to fill in your meal plan and then erase and redo each week!

Bad Meal Habit # 4 – I made the same old boring meals over and over again. Coming up with dinner ideas, especially at the last minute, can be hard. I was stuck in a rut of spaghetti, taco night, and soup and sandwiches for the longest time. Making dinner was always one of my least favorite chores and I struggled to come up with new quick and easy meal options. It wasn't until I took the time to make a "Master Meal List" that this all changed!

CHOOSING FROM AN ACTUAL PAPER LIST IS SO MUCH EASIER THAN TRYING TO MAKE A MENTAL ONE.

I took just a few minutes to make a master list of all our favorite meal options. This master list makes it quick and easy to meal plan as a family and now we choose meals that we probably wouldn't have thought of otherwise. In this chapter I have included our Meal Planning Helper for inspiration and a blank one for you and your family to fill out!

Bad Meal Habit #5 – I wasn't shopping my home. We had a freezer full of food, and yet nothing to actually eat for dinner. The problem was that we often had frozen meat, but nothing to pair it with or we were missing key ingredients that would have made a complete meal. Sound familiar?

Now, when meal planning, I do two things to ensure that we are not wasting food. First, I shop the freezer, fridge, and pantry for items that we can use in our weekly meals. I make sure to make note of the things we already have and try to work those into the meal plan before I fill out the grocery list. It's handy to have a **freezer inventory sheet** so you can quickly see at a glance what you have, without rummaging through the freezer. You will find a freezer inventory sheet here in this chapter!

Secondly, with five people in our family, we have two days remaining after we each choose one meal for the week. These two remaining days are perfect for "leftovers" and "freezer fixins." Leftovers are pretty obvious, but "freezer fixins" is a day where I use up all the lone items in the freezer or fridge and we have a hodgepodge of weirdness for dinner. Maybe there are only two burgers, a few chicken nuggets, some pizza pops and half a box of perogies in the freezer...not exactly a world class dinner, but my kids usually love this meal most of all. **It's a "use up what you have" meal and it does exactly that!** This meal is never pretty and it sure isn't going to be Pinterest worthy, but it's actually a fun and easy way to ensure that you aren't wasting food and money.

On the nights where we have scheduled leftovers or freezer fixins, but there are not any to be had, we treat ourselves to take-out! This is a great incentive for my family to eat leftovers for lunch and snacks throughout the week, pretty much ensuring that we get a weekly pizza/movie night as a family.

Bad Meal Habit #6 – I didn't have my recipes organized. Sure, I had cookbooks galore and even a few favorite meals written down...somewhere, but I could never find what I was looking for when I needed it. **One day I took about an hour to actually make myself a recipe binder and I let me tell you, it was *life-changing*.**

All of my favorite recipes are all in one place, sorted into categories and quick and easy to find. I used clear plastic sleeves to keep them clean and dry while cooking, and I love adding to my binder when I find a new recipe that I love. The best part? I was able to get rid of ALL my space-wasting cookbooks by writing out the few recipes I actually used, and then donating the books.

I am going to include some blank recipe pages for you in this book, along with some of my favorite recipes to get you started! You can either make a recipe binder (or a recipe box if you prefer) using the pages in the book. I like using a binder as a meal planner and recipe binder in one! You can store all of the pages from this chapter in your new binder along with all of your family's favorite recipes!

By organizing your meal planning, you are going to save time, money, and eat more healthy, home-cooked meals than ever before.

Don't forget that all of these pages are available for you to download for free and print at your convenience. I also recommend laminating your pages or putting them in clear plastic sleeves so that you can use them over and over again with a dry erase marker!

So, go ahead, start meal planning and create yourself a binder today.

Meal Planning

Shopping List

MONDAY

TUESDAY

WEDNESDAY

THURSDAY

FRIDAY

SATURDAY

SUNDAY

Meal Planning Helper

DINNER IDEAS THAT EVERYONE LOVES

LIST YOUR FAVORITE MEALS

1. Chicken & Dumplings
2. Chicken Fajitas
3. Chicken Alfredo
4. Chicken & Pineapple Kabobs
5. Orange Chicken & Rice
6. Chicken Stir Fry
7. Chicken Caesar Salad
8. Butter Chicken
9. Jambalaya
10. Taco Night
11. Spaghetti
12. Lasagna
13. Shepherd's Pie
14. Meatloaf & Mashed Potatoes
15. Roast Beef
16. Beef Stroganoff
17. Steak and Potatoes
18. Beef Stew
19. Pork Loin with Apple Glaze
20. Garlic Shrimp Pasta
21. Curry Fish & Veggies
22. Fish & Chips
23. Pierogies & Sausage
24. Homemade Pizza
25. Finger Foods
26.
27.
28.
29.
30.
31.

TEN-MINUTE MEALS

Cheese Quesadillas

Soup and Sandwiches

Pasta Marinara

Pizza Grilled Cheese

POTLUCK IDEAS

Deviled Eggs

Tex Mex Chili and Nachos

Sweet and Sour Meatballs

MEALS TO TRY

Meal Planning Helper

DINNER IDEAS THAT EVERYONE LOVES
LIST YOUR FAVORITE MEALS

1.
2.
3.
4.
5.
6.
7.
8.
9.
10.
11.
12.
13.
14.
15.
16.
17.
18.
19.
20.
21.
22.
23.
24.
25.
26.
27.
28.
29.
30.
31.

TEN-MINUTE MEALS

POTLUCK IDEAS

MEALS TO TRY

❧ Grocery List ❧

FRUITS
- [ ] Apples
- [ ] Bananas
- [ ] Grapes
- [ ] Oranges
- [ ] _____
- [ ] _____
- [ ] _____
- [ ] _____
- [ ] _____
- [ ] _____
- [ ] _____

VEGETABLES
- [ ] Carrots
- [ ] Lettuce
- [ ] Onion
- [ ] Spinach
- [ ] _____
- [ ] _____
- [ ] _____
- [ ] _____
- [ ] _____
- [ ] _____
- [ ] _____

PROTEIN
- [ ] Chicken Breast
- [ ] Ground Beef
- [ ] Pork Chops
- [ ] Salmon
- [ ] _____
- [ ] _____
- [ ] _____
- [ ] _____
- [ ] _____
- [ ] _____
- [ ] _____

DAIRY
- [ ] Butter
- [ ] Cheese
- [ ] Eggs
- [ ] Yogurt
- [ ] _____
- [ ] _____
- [ ] _____
- [ ] _____
- [ ] _____
- [ ] _____
- [ ] _____

FROZEN
- [ ] Ice Cream
- [ ] Peas & Carrots
- [ ] Pizza
- [ ] Meals
- [ ] _____
- [ ] _____
- [ ] _____
- [ ] _____
- [ ] _____
- [ ] _____
- [ ] _____

PANTRY
- [ ] Bagels
- [ ] Bread
- [ ] Cereal
- [ ] Pasta
- [ ] _____
- [ ] _____
- [ ] _____
- [ ] _____
- [ ] _____
- [ ] _____
- [ ] _____

CANNED GOODS
- [ ] Beans
- [ ] Chicken Broth
- [ ] Tomato Sauce
- [ ] Tuna
- [ ] _____
- [ ] _____
- [ ] _____
- [ ] _____
- [ ] _____
- [ ] _____
- [ ] _____

BEVERAGES
- [ ] Coffee
- [ ] Orange Juice
- [ ] Tea
- [ ] Water
- [ ] _____
- [ ] _____
- [ ] _____
- [ ] _____
- [ ] _____
- [ ] _____
- [ ] _____

OTHER
- [ ] Bleach
- [ ] Garbage Bags
- [ ] Paper Plates
- [ ] Pet Food
- [ ] _____
- [ ] _____
- [ ] _____
- [ ] _____
- [ ] _____
- [ ] _____

Grocery List

FRUITS
- [ ] Apples
- [ ] Bananas
- [ ] Grapes
- [ ] Oranges
- [ ] _____
- [ ] _____
- [ ] _____
- [ ] _____
- [ ] _____
- [ ] _____
- [ ] _____

VEGETABLES
- [ ] Carrots
- [ ] Lettuce
- [ ] Onion
- [ ] Spinach
- [ ] _____
- [ ] _____
- [ ] _____
- [ ] _____
- [ ] _____
- [ ] _____
- [ ] _____

PROTEIN
- [ ] Chicken Breast
- [ ] Ground Beef
- [ ] Pork Chops
- [ ] Salmon
- [ ] _____
- [ ] _____
- [ ] _____
- [ ] _____
- [ ] _____
- [ ] _____
- [ ] _____

DAIRY
- [ ] Butter
- [ ] Cheese
- [ ] Eggs
- [ ] Yogurt
- [ ] _____
- [ ] _____
- [ ] _____
- [ ] _____
- [ ] _____
- [ ] _____
- [ ] _____

FROZEN
- [ ] Ice Cream
- [ ] Peas & Carrots
- [ ] Pizza
- [ ] Meals
- [ ] _____
- [ ] _____
- [ ] _____
- [ ] _____
- [ ] _____
- [ ] _____
- [ ] _____

PANTRY
- [ ] Bagels
- [ ] Bread
- [ ] Cereal
- [ ] Pasta
- [ ] _____
- [ ] _____
- [ ] _____
- [ ] _____
- [ ] _____
- [ ] _____
- [ ] _____

CANNED GOODS
- [ ] Beans
- [ ] Chicken Broth
- [ ] Tomato Sauce
- [ ] Tuna
- [ ] _____
- [ ] _____
- [ ] _____
- [ ] _____
- [ ] _____
- [ ] _____
- [ ] _____

BEVERAGES
- [ ] Coffee
- [ ] Orange Juice
- [ ] Tea
- [ ] Water
- [ ] _____
- [ ] _____
- [ ] _____
- [ ] _____
- [ ] _____
- [ ] _____
- [ ] _____

OTHER
- [ ] Bleach
- [ ] Garbage Bags
- [ ] Paper Plates
- [ ] Pet Food
- [ ] _____
- [ ] _____
- [ ] _____
- [ ] _____
- [ ] _____
- [ ] _____
- [ ] _____

Party Planner

EVENT:_____

LOCATION:_____

DATE:_____ TIME:_____

NO. OF GUESTS:_____

Appetizers
_____
_____
_____
_____

Sides
_____
_____
_____
_____

Main Course
_____
_____
_____
_____

Desserts
_____
_____
_____
_____

Drinks
_____
_____
_____
_____

Other
_____
_____
_____
_____
_____
_____

Shopping List

- _____
- _____
- _____
- _____
- _____
- _____
- _____
- _____
- _____
- _____
- _____
- _____
- _____
- _____
- _____
- _____
- _____
- _____
- _____
- _____
- _____
- _____
- _____
- _____
- _____
- _____
- _____
- _____
- _____
- _____
- _____
- _____
- _____
- _____
- _____
- _____

Recipe Cards

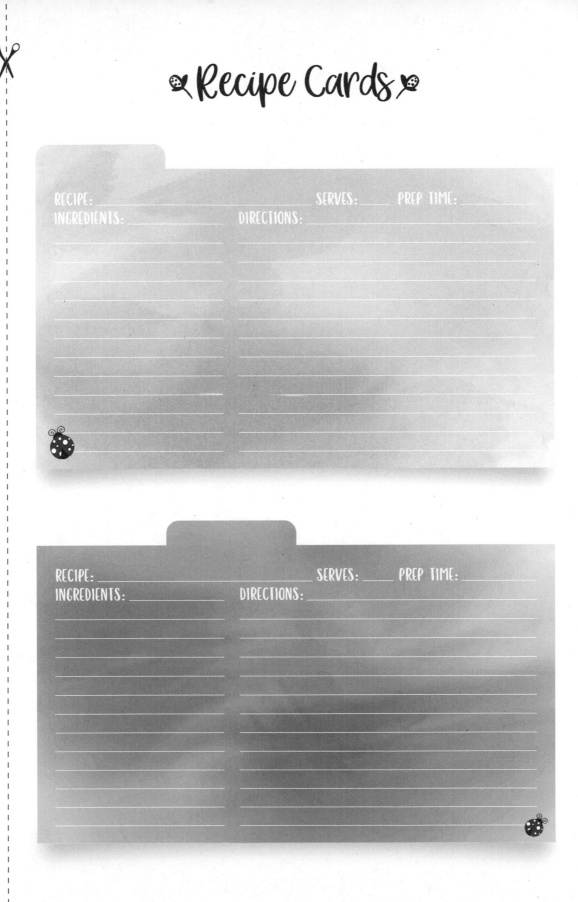

RECIPE: _____   SERVES: _____   PREP TIME: _____

INGREDIENTS: _____   DIRECTIONS: _____

RECIPE: _____   SERVES: _____   PREP TIME: _____

INGREDIENTS: _____   DIRECTIONS: _____

❧ Recipe Cards ❧

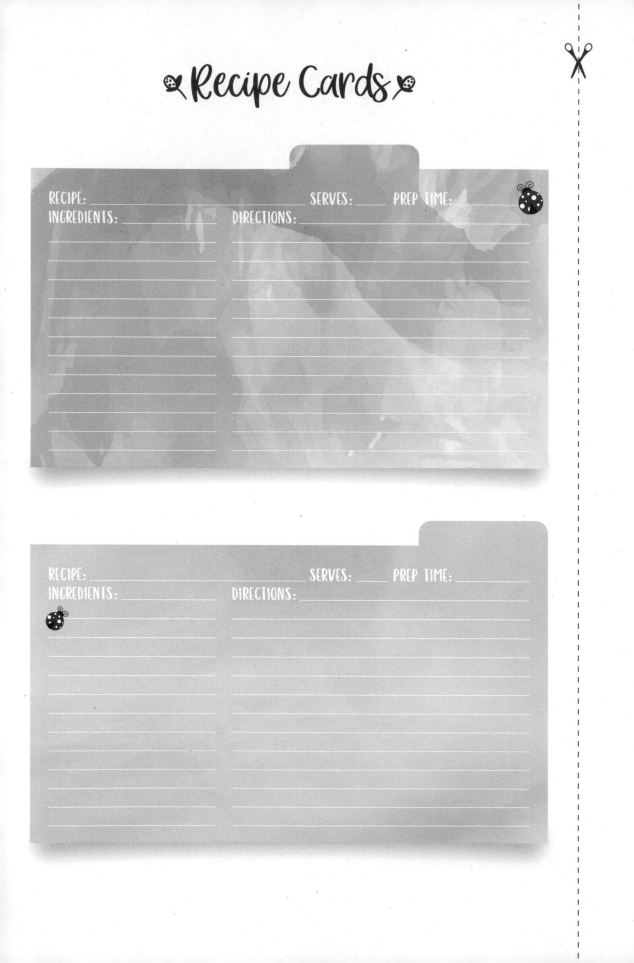

RECIPE: _____ SERVES: _____ PREP TIME: _____

INGREDIENTS: _____ DIRECTIONS: _____

RECIPE: _____ SERVES: _____ PREP TIME: _____

INGREDIENTS: _____ DIRECTIONS: _____

Recipe
Oprah's Chicken and Dumplings

CATEGORY: Dinner   SERVES: 6   PREP TIME: 15 min

INGREDIENTS:

2 lb. Boneless, Skinless Chicken

1 Medium Onion Chopped

2 Celery Ribs Chopped

4 Carrots Cut into Pieces

2 qt. Chicken Broth

Salt & Pepper to Taste

DUMPLINGS

1½ Cup All-Purpose Flour

2 Tbsp. of Oil

1 Cup Water

Optional: Parsley

DIRECTIONS:

Place chicken, broth, onion, celery, and carrots in large pot and bring to boil. Reduce heat and simmer for 45 minutes.

Mix flour and oil into bowl and gradually add water until dough becomes stiff. Roll out dough to ¼ inch thickness and cut into strips. Drop dough into simmering pot one at a time and avoid clumping. Simmer 8 minutes.

NOTES:

Serve with fresh bread and salad.

This soup reheats well and makes great leftovers.

✿ Recipe ✿ Easy Banana Bread

CATEGORY: Desserts   **SERVES:** 6   **PREP TIME:** 5 min

INGREDIENTS:

1½ Cup All-Purpose Flour	½ Cup Brown Sugar
1 tsp. Baking Soda	1 Egg
1 tsp. Baking Powder	2 Tbsp. of Milk
½ Cup Melted Butter	2 Over-Ripe Bananas
½ Cup White Sugar	Optional: A Sprinkle of Cloves, Cinnamon, and Nutmeg

DIRECTIONS:

Mix dry ingredients together in bowl.

Add melted butter, egg, and milk.

Mix in ripe bananas.

Heat oven to 350 degrees. Lightly grease pan.

40 minutes for bread pan / 23 minutes for muffin pan.

NOTES:

Makes 12 muffins or one loaf.

Recipe

CATEGORY: _____ SERVES: _____ PREP TIME: _____

INGREDIENTS:

_____ _____
_____ _____
_____ _____
_____ _____
_____ _____
_____ _____
_____ _____
_____ _____

DIRECTIONS:

_____
_____
_____
_____
_____
_____
_____
_____
_____
_____

NOTES:

_____
_____
_____
_____
_____
_____
_____
_____

❧ Recipe ❧ _____

CATEGORY: _____ SERVES: _____ PREP TIME: _____

INGREDIENTS:

_____ _____
_____ _____
_____ _____
_____ _____
_____ _____
_____ _____
_____ _____
_____ _____

DIRECTIONS:

_____
_____
_____
_____
_____
_____
_____
_____
_____
_____

NOTES:

_____
_____
_____
_____
_____
_____
_____
_____

❧ Coupon Organizer ❧

STORE:

ITEM		REG PRICE	SALE PRICE	COUPON VALUE	QTY	ITEM COST

STORE:

ITEM		REG PRICE	SALE PRICE	COUPON VALUE	QTY	ITEM COST

STORE:

ITEM		REG PRICE	SALE PRICE	COUPON VALUE	QTY	ITEM COST

Freezer Inventory

MEATS

QTY	ITEM	DATE

SEAFOOD

QTY	ITEM	DATE

DELI

QTY	ITEM	DATE

FRUITS

QTY	ITEM	DATE

VEGETABLES

QTY	ITEM	DATE

GRAINS

QTY	ITEM	DATE

BAKED GOODS

QTY	ITEM	DATE

MEALS

QTY	ITEM	DATE

OTHER

QTY	ITEM	DATE

≋ Chapter Six ≋

ORGANIZING YOUR FINANCES

HOW TO BUDGET, SAVE, AND MAKE YOUR MONEY WORK FOR YOU.

Talking about your personal financial situation can be uncomfortable and I rarely discuss mine with anyone. The truth is, **most** of us avoid talking about money, whether it's the struggles or even the successes. It just seems a bit taboo. The downside of keeping our personal finances a secret is that we are not sharing our advice, tips, or knowledge with each other. As a child, my parents never discussed our family's personal financial situation, and basic money management wasn't taught in school either. **How can we possibly learn the ins and outs of money without education, communication, or support?**

≫

MANAGING MONEY, LIKE MOST THINGS IN LIFE, REQUIRES KNOWLEDGE AND ORGANIZATION.

≪

My only knowledge of money was that you needed it to buy stuff and that you earned it with the sole purpose of spending it. From about the age of nineteen until my mid twenties, I worked two or three jobs at a time, which averaged over sixty hours per week. I was living in a tiny bachelor apartment, I did not own a car and I had very little furniture or possessions to call my own. Despite my meagre living conditions and non-stop work hours, I was in debt up to my eyeballs.

At the age of twenty-five, I was finally forced to declare bankruptcy. I had crushing amounts of debt and very little to actually show for it. How did I get into such a terrible financial situation so young? Credit cards. I got my first credit card at the age of nineteen and I remember I was like a kid at Christmas! After living on my own and being extremely poor in my late teens, a credit card seemed like the answer to my prayers. I could finally afford to buy new clothes, basic household necessities, and I no longer had to worry about where my next meal was coming from. I thought my credit card meant the end to my financial struggles.

Sure, I paid my minimum monthly credit card payments, but I never paid off the balance, and each month it continued to grow. I was completely elated one day while shopping at a retail store, when the cashier offered me an instant store credit card, which came with an extra ten percent off my purchase. I happily accepted and before I knew it, I had signed up for three or four more store cards that I was also making minimum payments on.

The final straw was a trip to a furniture store where I purchased a new sofa and television set on their "payment plan," which promised me a small monthly payment in exchange for some awesome brand-new stuff.

⇶

SMALL PURCHASES, WITH SMALL INTEREST PAYMENTS CAN QUICKLY ADD UP TO A BIG AND OVERWHELMING AMOUNT OF DEBT.

⫷

You are probably shaking your head. How could I not know the consequences of my misuse of credit? **The truth is, I really was completely oblivious to how credit even worked**. I had never even *heard* of compound interest, let alone understood the fundamentals. I really thought that the minimum monthly payments were all that I was required to pay, so I continued doing just that.

The problem was that those minimum payments were barely covering the interest, and at twenty percent for the retail credit cards and even more for the furniture loan, the interest payments were causing my debt balance to grow at an exponential rate.

Here is an example of how interest can crush you. The new sofa I purchased was $500 and the television set was another $250. At the time, $750 seemed like a lot of money and so, instead of saving for it, I opted for the "buy now, pay later" approach and used the store's "low monthly payment plan." With a payment of only $30 a month for 5 years, it seemed so much more affordable! Of course, I signed on the dotted line and took home my new furniture without a second thought.

If I had taken the time to actually do the math, I would have realized that I was paying $1800 for $750 worth of things. That seems crazy, doesn't it? Who in their right mind would do such a thing? The answer is, unfortunately, **most people**.

Perhaps it isn't as obvious as spending over $1,000 more for a sofa than it's worth, but every time we carry a credit card balance month to month, we are paying interest on our purchases, which costs us even more of our hard-earned money.

Every time we make a minimum payment on our credit card or loan, most, if not all of that money, is just going towards the interest. As we continue to make purchases, even when paying the monthly bill, our debt continues to grow. Before you know it, your monthly payments can take away a huge portion of your pay check, **without those payments even touching your actual debt.**

For me, the loss of a job was all it took for my money-balancing act to come tumbling down. I had zero savings and no idea how I was going to pay my rent, let alone make my monthly debt payments. When you live pay check to pay check and you suddenly are no longer receiving a pay check, well, the reality of your poor financial decisions will really hit home.

There is hope. The key to becoming debt-free and finally having financial security is having a little bit of knowledge and organization. When I first met my now husband, he quickly schooled me in the art of money management. Trust me, I was not an ideal student. With zero understanding of how money worked and even less self discipline, I struggled to "live below my means" at first. "What?? I have to wait until my next payday before buying this awesome shirt that is on sale now???" My husband made me read books like *Rich Dad, Poor Dad* and *The Wealthy Barber*, which I highly recommend for anyone looking to transform their financial situation and learn the basics of growing your personal wealth.

With a little bit of knowledge, I was able to then focus on getting my finances organized. I'll never forget the first time I made a monthly budget; I couldn't believe how much money I SHOULD have had left over each month after paying my fixed bills...but, where was it all going?

≫

MY MONTHLY BUDGET OPENED MY EYES TO HOW MUCH MONEY I WAS WASTING EACH MONTH WITHOUT EVEN REALIZING IT.

≪

In this chapter, you will find a **Family Budget Worksheet** where you can enter in your monthly income and expenses. You can download the **Cluttered Mess to Organized Success Worksheets** for free with your promo code.

Once I finished my monthly budget, I was determined to find out where the extra money was going! I spent one entire month tracking my spending. **I wrote down every purchase I made, and let me tell you, it was financial death by a thousand paper cuts.** You will not believe how fast five dollars at a coffee shop a few times a week, or a weekly trip to the dollar store, can add up to hundreds of dollars a month! I was shocked at how quickly all these tiny purchases added up to a huge chunk of my income. Once aware, I became more cautious of each dollar I spent.

This chapter includes a spending tracker, savings tracker, debt tracker, and a monthly bills reminder worksheet that you can use to organize all of your finances quickly and easily.

WANTS VERSUS NEANDS

➤➤➤

IN ORDER TO REALLY DIG YOURSELF OUT OF DEBT AND GAIN FINANCIAL FREEDOM, YOU ARE GOING TO HAVE TO MAKE SOME TOUGH SACRIFICES...AND IT'S GOING TO SUCK SOMETIMES.

≪≪

My husband and I decided to save money by becoming a one-vehicle family. Because he traveled for work, my husband got the car most of the time. I spent **FIVE YEARS** pulling my children (and my daycare children) to the grocery store in multiple wagons tied together with ropes. I called it my "ghetto train," and it was a sight to be seen. **I would pull three wagons tied together, filled with small children and loaded with groceries, while I pushed a double stroller (complete with two babies) with the other hand.** I pulled my train and pushed that stroller to doctor's appointments, grocery stores and everywhere else we needed to go. I pulled and pushed my contraption through the pouring rain and freezing snow, and I hated every minute of it.

I wanted a second vehicle. But with monthly car payments, gas, and insurance, the cost of that WANT wasn't worth it. **We spent five years focusing on our family's NEEDS, (monthly bills, food, clothing), and denying ourselves a lot of WANTS (second vehicle, cable, cell phone, vacations, etc.).** At the end of just five short years, we were debt-free and we had saved enough money for a six-month emergency fund (in case my husband ever lost his job). We also started investing ten percent of our money each month into a retirement fund. **I had learned how compound**

interest could work *for us*, instead of *against us* like with credit cards, which meant our money was now *earning* us even more money each month.

Financial freedom isn't going to happen overnight. It will take time and discipline, but it will be so worth it. You will find many worksheets in this chapter that can help you get well on your way to understanding and organizing your money, and that is half the battle.

Here are five steps I recommend for money management success!

- **Step One: Make a budget**
- **Step Two: Track your spending**
- **Step Three: Pay down your debt (smallest debt first)**
- **Step Four: Start an emergency fund (3 months worth of bills)**
- **Step Five: Invest 10 percent of your income for retirement**

Of course, these steps are really simplified and they will take time, practice, and hard work to implement, but every step you take—no matter how small—will put you one step closer.

I have also included in this chapter some tips for organizing and filing your paperwork. Paper clutter is the number one complaint I get from clients and people who follow my blog. **Let's be honest, a big reason why people struggle with paper clutter is that they just have no idea of what they are supposed to keep and what they aren't!** Monthly bills, credit card statements, tax information, and other financial papers can add up to a lot of clutter fast and the thought of getting rid of important financial papers can cause a lot of fear. **Don't let your paper push you around!** Create yourself a short and a long term filing system that will get your paper clutter under control once and for all. You will find a worksheet to help you organize your papers properly in this chapter. You can also use the premade file folder labels in Chapter Ten to create yourself an organized paper filing system quickly and easily.

So, what are you waiting for? Take the first step to Financial Success and fill out these financial worksheets today.

DEBT IS NORMAL—BE WEIRD.

QUICK AND EASY MONEY-SAVING TIPS

- Get rid of cable or satellite and choose Netflix instead.
- Shop your insurance company and you could save hundreds a year.
- Switch your bank account to one that has lower or zero monthly fees.
- Use the Flipp app or flyers to price match when grocery shopping.
- The 24 Rule. Wait 24 hours before making any purchases of "wants" over $24.
- Always make a shopping list before going to the grocery store and stick to it.
- Cook double the meat for "one meat—two meals" at least once a week (find some recipe examples in Chapter Five).
- Get a library card and use it for movies, books and audiobooks.
- Do the 7-Day Challenge every few months. Spend NOTHING for 7 days. Not one dime. Stock up on groceries and fill your gas tank before you start.
- Shop second-hand. When you want something, see if you can find the same item gently used first from online swap sites.
- Never buy a brand-new vehicle. Ask dealerships about demos, which still come with warranties, but with a much lower price tag.
- Setup a babysitter swap program with your friends and neighbors.
- Make your own DIY cleaning products. You can find my favorite recipes in Chapter Four of this book.
- Get handy! Watch YouTube videos to learn how to do small repair or home improvement jobs all by yourself.
- Sell your unused items on online swap sites. Make some extra money and declutter your space at the same time.

CUT OUT THIS CARD AND TAPE IT IN YOUR WALLET.

DO I REALLY NEED THIS?

DO I HAVE SPACE FOR THIS?

WILL THIS PURCHASE BRING ME HAPPINESS LONG TERM?

If you answer "no" to any of these questions, do the right thing and put it back!

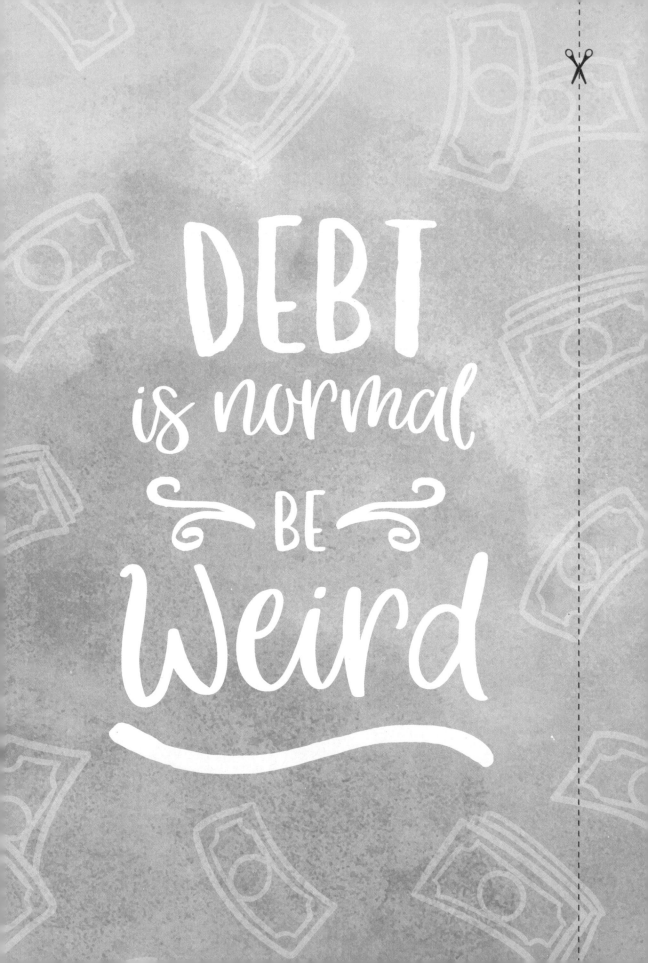

Track Your Spending

GET ON TRACK!

DATE	DETAILS	AMOUNT	TOTAL
/ /			
/ /			
/ /			
/ /			
/ /			
/ /			
/ /			
/ /			
/ /			
/ /			
/ /			
/ /			
/ /			
/ /			
/ /			
/ /			
/ /			
/ /			
/ /			
/ /			
/ /			
/ /			
/ /			

Year at a Glance

FAMILY FINANCIAL PLANNER

JANUARY
Income _____
Expenses _____
Giving _____
Saving _____
Loans _____

FEBRUARY
Income _____
Expenses _____
Giving _____
Saving _____
Loans _____

MARCH
Income _____
Expenses _____
Giving _____
Saving _____
Loans _____

APRIL
Income _____
Expenses _____
Giving _____
Saving _____
Loans _____

MAY
Income _____
Expenses _____
Giving _____
Saving _____
Loans _____

JUNE
Income _____
Expenses _____
Giving _____
Saving _____
Loans _____

JULY
Income _____
Expenses _____
Giving _____
Saving _____
Loans _____

AUGUST
Income _____
Expenses _____
Giving _____
Saving _____
Loans _____

SEPTEMBER
Income _____
Expenses _____
Giving _____
Saving _____
Loans _____

OCTOBER
Income _____
Expenses _____
Giving _____
Saving _____
Loans _____

NOVEMBER
Income _____
Expenses _____
Giving _____
Saving _____
Loans _____

DECEMBER
Income _____
Expenses _____
Giving _____
Saving _____
Loans _____

Savings Tracker

SAVING JUST $5 A DAY IS ALMOST $2,000 A YEAR!

DATE	DETAILS	AMOUNT	TOTAL
/ /			
/ /			
/ /			
/ /			
/ /			
/ /			
/ /			
/ /			
/ /			
/ /			
/ /			
/ /			
/ /			
/ /			
/ /			
/ /			
/ /			
/ /			
/ /			
/ /			
/ /			
/ /			
/ /			
/ /			
/ /			

❧ Monthly Bills ❧
& Expenses Reminder

DO YOU SOMETIMES FORGET A BILL?
WRITE THEM DOWN AND CHECK THEM OFF!

BILL						
AMOUNT						
DUE						
JANUARY						
FEBRUARY						
MARCH						
APRIL						
MAY						
JUNE						
JULY						
AUGUST						
SEPTEMBER						
OCTOBER						
NOVEMBER						
DECEMBER						
TOTAL						

❧ Loans and Debts Tracker ❧

GET DEBT-FREE FAST! PAY THE LOWEST DEBT OFF FIRST.

LOAN	AMOUNT	% RATE	PAYMENT	BALANCE	GOAL Ø	NOTES

❧ Family Budget Worksheet ❧

EXPENSES	WEEKLY	MONTHLY	YEARLY
Mortgage and Taxes	$	$	$
Insurance	$	$	$
Electricity	$	$	$
Gas	$	$	$
Water	$	$	$
Home Phone	$	$	$
Internet	$	$	$
Cell Phones	$	$	$
Groceries	$	$	$
Restaurants and Fast Food	$	$	$
Car Payment	$	$	$
Gas	$	$	$
Car Insurance	$	$	$
Car Maintenance	$	$	$
	$	$	$
	$	$	$
	$	$	$
SAVING & INVESTMENTS			
To Be Saved	$	$	$
	$	$	$
	$	$	$
GIFTS AND CHARITY			
Christmas	$	$	$
Birthdays	$	$	$
	$	$	$
MEDICAL			
Check-ups	$	$	$
Prescriptions	$	$	$
	$	$	$
ENTERTAINMENT EXPENSES			
Clothing	$	$	$
	$	$	$
	$	$	$
	$	$	$
TOTAL EXPENSES	$	$	$

🌿 Family Budget Worksheet 🌿

EXPENSES	WEEKLY	MONTHLY	YEARLY
Employment Income	$	$	$
Other Income	$	$	$
	$	$	$
	$	$	$
	$	$	$
	$	$	$
SAVING & INVESTMENTS			
Investment Income	$	$	$
	$	$	$
	$	$	$
	$	$	$
	$	$	$
GIFTS AND CHARITY			
Gifts	$	$	$
	$	$	$
	$	$	$
	$	$	$
	$	$	$
TOTAL INCOME	$	$	$
TOTAL NET INCOME	$	$	$

A penny saved is a penny earned.

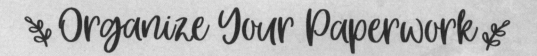

Organize Your Paperwork

SORT AND FILE YOUR PAPERWORK INTO SHORT TERM, LONG TERM, AND DISCARD FILES

LONG-TERM PAPERS

- Appliance manuals, warranties, and service contracts
- Yearly bank statements
- Credit card contracts
- Legal documents
- Education records, diploma, transcripts, etc.
- Employment records
- Family health records, including vaccination histories
- Health benefit information
- Income tax papers (last 7 years only)
- Insurance policies
- Yearly loan statements
- Password list
- Receipts for items under warranty
- Safe deposit box inventory (and key)
- Tax receipts, such as those received for charitable deductions

SHORT-TERM PAPERS

- Monthly bank statements
- Bill payment receipts
- Bills awaiting payment
- Monthly credit card statements
- Misc "To-Do" papers

DISCARD

- Cancelled checks for cash or nondeductible expenses
- Expired warranties
- Pay stubs, after reconciling with W-2
- Income tax papers over 7 years old
- Monthly bills and statements over 12 months old

❧ Paper Purging Guide ❧

HOW LONG DO YOU NEED TO KEEP IMPORTANT PAPERS?

DOCUMENTS	HOW LONG TO KEEP IT
Bank statements	1 year, unless needed to support tax filings
Birth certificates, marriage licenses, divorce decrees, passports, education records, military service records	Forever
Contracts	Until updated
Credit card records	Until paid, unless needed to support tax filings
Home purchase and improvement records	As long as you own the property
Household inventory	Forever; update as needed
Insurance, life	Forever
Insurance, car, home, etc.	Until you renew the policy
Investment statements	Shred your monthly statements; keep annual statements until you sell the investments
Investment certificates	Until you cash or sell the item
Loan documents	Until you sell the item the loan was for
Real estate deeds	As long as you own the property
Receipts for large purchases	Until you sell or discard the item
Service contracts and warranties	Until you sell or discard the item
Social Insurance Card	Forever
Marriage Certificate	Forever
Tax records	7 years from the filing date
Vehicle titles	Until you sell or dispose of the car
Will	Until updated

My Buy Wish List
SAVE FOR SOMETHING SPECIAL

PAID!	I'M SAVING FOR...	BUDGET

⪦ Chapter Seven ⪧

ORGANIZING YOUR HEALTH

HOW TO BE A HEALTHIER AND HAPPIER YOU.

Living a healthy lifestyle is something I struggle with, but I have come a long way on my journey, and I now make my health more of a priority in my life. While researching this chapter, I was incredibly inspired by so many people who make their health a top priority and use organization to help make it happen. I was geeked to find that not only do the top fitness gurus share their success on social media, but they share the printables that helped them to achieve their health and fitness goals too. I have gathered the very best organizing tools I could find to help you live a more healthy and active lifestyle (and me right along with you). I am also including some important health worksheets that just may save your life (or someone you love).

The truth is, if you are like me and suffer from some medical issues, this chapter is probably the most important one in the entire book. It's critical that your family have access to information about your current medical conditions, what medication you take (and the dosage), what vitamins you take, your blood type, and your family medical history in case of an emergency. It's also important that you have access to your entire family's medical information, even for extended family, like parents and siblings.

A few years ago, we had a horrible health scare in our family. Without going into too many personal details, a close family member was rushed to the hospital in critical condition. While doctors frantically worked to save this family members life, we were asked a series of critical questions about medications, dosages and past medical conditions...none of which we had the answers to. Thankfully, this family member made a full recovery, but this experience taught me a valuable lesson on the importance of being prepared.

>>>

ARE YOU PREPARED
FOR A FAMILY MEDICAL EMERGENCY?

<<<

With aging parents and loved ones, I think it's a great idea to have a copy of their medical information in case of an emergency, especially if you are their next of kin. Knowing the medications they take, allergies they have, and family medical history could just help save their life. In this chapter, you will find a **medical information sheet** that you can fill out for yourself and everyone in your family. Photocopy, or print extra copies and ask loved ones to fill them out for you to hold onto. While this may seem like an invasion of privacy to some, it really can open the doors to learning about your own family medical history and give you valuable information if there is ever a medical emergency.

I am a crazy freak about updating my medical information sheet and making sure my husband has memorized the darn thing. Not only am I a slight hypochondriac, but I have had a host of weird medical issues that have scared the crap out of me, so I'm always prepared for the next one! Pregnancy and I didn't get along very well. With all three of my pregnancies I had some health issues, which all required that my husband be fully informed in case of an emergency. With Izzy, I had placenta previa (which ruptured) and was placed on bed rest when I was only three months pregnant. I literally stayed in bed and watched movies for the majority of my entire first pregnancy. Laying in bed for seven months straight is not nearly as awesome as it sounds. With Abby, my growing baby belly was invading my heart space and I fainted...a lot. At the grocery store, while cutting the grass...basically anytime I did anything even remotely physical. I wore a heart monitor for an entire month and I had to visit the cardiologist weekly. Fun times.

My third and final pregnancy was the scariest of all. I was severely anemic and had something called ITP. That is short for a big, long term bleeding disorder that basically means my blood didn't clot. I had regular blood transfusions and steroid injections to try and bring my platelets levels up, but they remained dangerously low during the last two months of my pregnancy. My doctor basically told me not to bang my head or cut myself, and if I did, I was to go to the emergency room immediately. I wanted to bubble wrap myself. For someone already suffering from a bad case of clumsy, I was certain it was the end and that I was going to croak at any given moment. I used to playfully yell "I'm coming Martha" (yeah, I'm THAT old) every time I stubbed my toe or bumped into something.

My poor husband, I was **constantly** reminding him that he had to "bring my medical binder" if I was ever in an accident or went into early labor. Ultimately, everything turned out fine and I was back to my old scab-making self soon after Milo was born!

>>>

IF NOTHING ELSE, THOSE MEDICAL INFORMATION SHEETS GAVE ME SOME MUCH-NEEDED PEACE OF MIND DURING THOSE STRESSFUL TIMES.

<<<

Besides your medical information sheet, a **medical benefits sheet** is important to have if you or your loved ones are ever admitted into the hospital. I'll never forget the day I was trying to fill out the paperwork for an extended family member who was being admitted into the hospital in an emergency situation. I had no idea about health benefits nor did I have access to their health card number. During this stressful time, it would have been a blessing to have this information, instead of having to ask their overwhelmed and emotional spouse to fill out the paperwork.

I now have a **"family medical section"** in my household management binder, where I keep all of these important medical information sheets for my entire family. I also use clear plastic sleeves in the binder where I slide in copies of recent medical test results and prescription receipts too. I also store my children's immunization cards and records in my binder. You can use the pages in this chapter to create a "Family Medical Binder" or heck, just fill out the pages and bring this entire book in case of an emergency! I have also included a wellness tracker in this chapter (just for kids), so you can to track their growth and record their immunizations.

The best thing about having all your medical information in one convenient spot is that, if there ever was an emergency, a family member or neighbor could quickly grab your information and relay the information over the phone!

⇶

TAKE A STEP TOWARDS A HEALTHIER, HAPPIER YOU.

⇷

On a more positive note, let's talk about how organization can help us achieve a more active and healthier lifestyle!

Let's be honest, being active is an important part of being healthy, and it is something we should all make a priority. In our busy and hectic lives, finding extra time in the day can be hard, and that is where organization comes in. In this chapter, you are going to find some great organizing tools that can help you plan your physical activity, set goals and keep yourself on track and accountable!

Whether your health goals are to lose weight, gain muscle or just improve your overall health, you will find a lot of helpful worksheets to get you organized and help you achieve your fitness goals!

I spend a whole lot of time telling myself a host of excuses as to why I don't work out. Unfortunately, excuses don't burn calories! For me, lack of time is the number one excuse I tell myself on a daily basis. **Truth be told, a one-hour work out is less that four percent of my entire day**. I can find just four percent of my day to do something that is going to extend my life and make me happier! I *need* to find the time...and so do you.

↠

LET'S COMMIT TO BEING FIT NOW!

⇜

I'm going to stop making excuses and start making changes. **My butt isn't going to get any smaller by sitting on it!** To get started, we have to begin by writing down our fitness goals (see chapter one for the reasons why goal setting will help you succeed). **Once a goal is set, you are well on your way to a plan.**

Now it's time to organize and plan for fitness success. Fortunately, the planning and organizing part does not involve sweating, but is still a critical part of a healthy lifestyle.

So, grab a pen and let's get started. I love the fitness planning pages in this chapter, I find them so inspiring, and I hope that you will too! Don't forget, all the pages in this chapter are available for you to print at home as part of your free download!

❧ Family Medical Information ❧

Name: _____

Primary Doctor Name and Telephone Number: _____

Health Card Number: _____

Health Insurance Number: _____

Emergency Contact Name and Relationship: _____

Telephone Number: _____

Blood Type: _____

Allergies: (List any medications or food allergies that you have and your reaction.)

_____

_____

MEDICATIONS: (List all prescription and over the counter medications you are currently taking.)

Medication	Dose	Purpose/Treatment

VITAMINS: (List all vitamins and supplements.)

Name	Quantity/Purpose

MEDICAL HISTORY: (List all past surgeries and medical issues.)

Surgery	Date/Reason

Medical Issues	Date/Explanation

Family History	Illness/Paternal or Maternal Side

Medical Benefits Information

Your Name: _____

Cell phone: _____ Work phone: _____

Email: _____ Date of birth: _____

Benefits company: _____

Health card number: _____

Policy number: _____

Your company: _____

Address: _____

_____

Supervisor: _____

Partner's Name: _____

Cell phone: _____ Work phone: _____

Email: _____ Date of birth: _____

Benefits company: _____

Health card number: _____

Policy number: _____

Partner's company: _____

Address: _____

_____

Supervisor: _____

❦ Family History ❦

MOTHER'S SIDE

	NAME	BIRTH DATE	ILLNESS/CONDITION	AGE/CAUSE OF DEATH
GRANDPA				
GRANDMA				
SIBLING				
SIBLING				

FATHER'S SIDE

	NAME	BIRTH DATE	ILLNESS/CONDITION	AGE/CAUSE OF DEATH
GRANDPA				
GRANDMA				
SIBLING				
SIBLING				

MY FAMILY

	NAME	BIRTH DATE	ILLNESS/CONDITION	AGE/CAUSE OF DEATH
ME				
SIBLING				
SIBLING				
SIBLING				
SIBLING				

Wellness Check Ups

NAME: _____

AGE	DATE	HEIGHT	WEIGHT	NOTES

VACCINATIONS

DATE	NAME	DATE	NAME

Fitness Goals

FOR THE MONTH OF:

_____

MY FITNESS GOALS FOR THIS MONTH:

○ WALKING   ○ RUNNING   ○ YOGA   ○ WEIGHTS   ○ _____   ○ _____

I AM DOING WELL WITH _____

_____

I NEED TO IMPROVE ON _____

_____

MY STRENGTHS ARE _____

_____

MY WEAKNESSES ARE _____

_____

MY WORKOUT DAYS ARE _____

MY REST DAYS ARE _____

60-SECOND FITNESS TEST

How many of each exercise can you
do in 60 seconds?

	BEGINNING OF THE MONTH	END OF THE MONTH
SIT-UPS	_____	_____
PUSH-UPS	_____	_____
JUMPING JACKS	_____	_____
BURPEES	_____	_____

❧ Fitness Goals ❧
FOR THE MONTH OF:

_____

MY FITNESS GOALS FOR THIS MONTH:

○ WALKING   ○ RUNNING   ○ YOGA   ○ WEIGHTS   ○ _____   ○ _____

I AM DOING WELL WITH _____

_____

I NEED TO IMPROVE ON _____

_____

MY STRENGTHS ARE _____

_____

MY WEAKNESSES ARE _____

_____

MY WORKOUT DAYS ARE _____

MY REST DAYS ARE _____

60-SECOND FITNESS TEST

How many of each exercise can you
do in 60 seconds?

	BEGINNING OF THE MONTH	END OF THE MONTH
SIT-UPS	_____	_____
PUSH-UPS	_____	_____
JUMPING JACKS	_____	_____
BURPEES	_____	_____

Health and Fitness Goals
WEEKLY CHECKLIST

	S	M	T	W	T	F	S
Drink 32 oz. + Water	○	○	○	○	○	○	○
Exercise 30 + Minutes	○	○	○	○	○	○	○
Three Servings Fruit/Veggies	○	○	○	○	○	○	○
No Eating After 9 p.m.	○	○	○	○	○	○	○
No Treats on Weekdays	○	○	○	○	○	○	○
One Treat on Weekends	○	○	○	○	○	○	○

	S	M	T	W	T	F	S
Drink 32 oz. + Water	○	○	○	○	○	○	○
Exercise 30 + Minutes	○	○	○	○	○	○	○
Three Servings Fruit/Veggies	○	○	○	○	○	○	○
No Eating After 9 p.m.	○	○	○	○	○	○	○
No Treats on Weekdays	○	○	○	○	○	○	○
One Treat on Weekends	○	○	○	○	○	○	○

	S	M	T	W	T	F	S
Drink 32 oz. + Water	○	○	○	○	○	○	○
Exercise 30 + Minutes	○	○	○	○	○	○	○
Three Servings Fruit/Veggies	○	○	○	○	○	○	○
No Eating After 9 p.m.	○	○	○	○	○	○	○
No Treats on Weekdays	○	○	○	○	○	○	○
One Treat on Weekends	○	○	○	○	○	○	○

❧ Overcome Your Obstacles ❧

OBSTACLE:

Ideas/Steps to Overcome

OBSTACLE:

Ideas/Steps to Overcome

OBSTACLE:

Ideas/Steps to Overcome

OBSTACLE:

Ideas/Steps to Overcome

"It's not about having time, it's about making time."

❦ Before ❦   ❦ After ❦

PICTURE HERE

PICTURE HERE

AREA OF CONCERN

AREA OF CONCERN

Starting Date: _____
Weight: _____
Neck: _____
Bust: _____
Waist: _____
Bicep: _____
Hips: _____
Thigh: _____
Calf: _____

Starting Date: _____
Weight: _____
Neck: _____
Bust: _____
Waist: _____
Bicep: _____
Hips: _____
Thigh: _____
Calf: _____

NOTES

NOTES

Workout Schedule

MONDAY

TUESDAY

WEDNESDAY

THURSDAY

FRIDAY

SATURDAY

SUNDAY

NOTES

❧ Workout Log ❧

DATE:

Activity	Time	Distance	Sets	Reps	Weight

DATE:

Activity	Time	Distance	Sets	Reps	Weight

DATE:

Activity	Time	Distance	Sets	Reps	Weight

DATE:

Activity	Time	Distance	Sets	Reps	Weight

NOTES: _____

_____

_____

SORE today STRONG tomorrow

🌿 Progress Tracker 🌿
MEASUREMENT PROGRESS

Week	Neck	Bust	Waist	Hips	Bicep	Thigh	Calf
1							
2							
3							
4							
5							
6							
7							
8							
9							
10							
11							
12							

WEIGHT LOSS/GAIN PROGRESS

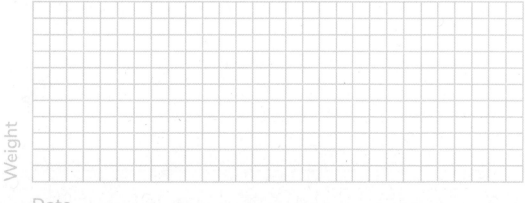

Weight

Date

❧ Vitamins & Supplements ❧

MONTH: _____

VITAMINS/SUPPLEMENTS:

	S	M	T	W	T	F	S
_____	○	○	○	○	○	○	○
_____	○	○	○	○	○	○	○
_____	○	○	○	○	○	○	○
_____	○	○	○	○	○	○	○
_____	○	○	○	○	○	○	○
_____	○	○	○	○	○	○	○
_____	○	○	○	○	○	○	○
_____	○	○	○	○	○	○	○
_____	○	○	○	○	○	○	○
_____	○	○	○	○	○	○	○
_____	○	○	○	○	○	○	○
_____	○	○	○	○	○	○	○
_____	○	○	○	○	○	○	○
_____	○	○	○	○	○	○	○
_____	○	○	○	○	○	○	○
_____	○	○	○	○	○	○	○
_____	○	○	○	○	○	○	○
_____	○	○	○	○	○	○	○
_____	○	○	○	○	○	○	○

NOTES: _____

_____

_____

≷ Chapter Eight ≷

ORGANIZING FOR
EMERGENCIES

HOW TO PLAN AND BE PREPARED FOR THE WORST-CASE SCENARIO.

As I get older, I have become much more of a realist. My rose-colored glasses must have gotten lost in the clutter somewhere along the way because, while I'm still pretty optimistic and positive, I know that bad stuff happens when you least expect it, and now I'm much more prepared.

Life isn't perfect. Mistakes happen, loved ones pass away, illnesses strike, jobs are lost, houses are destroyed, and sometimes crap just goes horribly, insanely wrong. Such is the story of life.

While I truly believe that we should all focus on the positive things in life, I also believe it's important not to ignore the potential bad stuff that will *eventually* come our way.

≫

DENIAL AND IGNORANCE DO NOTHING BUT MAKE BAD SITUATIONS WORSE.

≪

We have all heard the saying "plan for the worst and hope for the best," but how many of us actually have a plan for life's worst-case scenarios? Most of us never even *think* about illness, death, job loss, or natural disasters, let alone plan for them. If we are *really* honest with ourselves, we know that something craptacular is going to happen sooner or later, and being prepared can make these rough times a little bit easier.

In this chapter, we will be planning for those unexpected and unfortunate things that life can sometimes suddenly throw at us. By filling out these pages and completing these checklists, you are going to be ready for anything, or at the very least, feel more in control in an out-of-control situation.

What if your basement suddenly floods? No worries! You will have your insurance policy number and contact information at your fingertips in minutes. What if you get hit by a bus tomorrow and suddenly pass away? Your family will be thankful you took the time to fill out these emergency-planning pages so they can easily find everything they need. Zombie Apocalypse? I got you! Your **Emergency Checklist** will ensure you have everything you need to wait out the biters in the safety of your home (well, at least for the first seventy-two hours).

In all seriousness though, being prepared is what organization is all about. I'm not suggesting that you start digging a bunker or hoarding canned goods, but there are some quick and easy things you can do to make the bad stuff a little less awful. Not only are you going to be more prepared for the crazy that is life, but these pages are going to give you some much-needed peace of mind as well.

Take just a few minutes to fill out the **emergency guide and emergency contact list** and save yourself from having to frantically look up phone numbers in stressful situations. I highly recommend using the contact page to add the information of your utility companies (like electricity, phone, internet) in case you ever have issues with your service and need to contact them right away. **Also, add the phone numbers of your auto mechanic, plumber, electrician, veterinarian, lawyer, accountant, and other contacts that you or a family member may need to get in touch with quickly.**

>>>

IT TURNS OUT BEING AN ADULT IS LIKE LOOKING BOTH WAYS BEFORE YOU CROSS THE STREET AND THEN GETTING HIT BY AN AIRPLANE.

<<<

There are a few things that every adult needs to do as part of basic adulting 101. I have included an **Adulting 101 checklist** in this chapter to help guide you in the ways of all things "grown-up." I still feel like a teenager trapped in a forty-year-old body, but now that I have kids of my own, it's imperative that I have completed all the things on this checklist for their sake.

When I was twenty-six years old, my first daughter, Izzy, was born. A few months later, my husband dragged me to a lawyer to get our wills and power of attorneys drawn up. Joe has always been the responsible half of this partnership, while I prefer to simply fly by the seat of my pants. I felt silly getting a will when we had hardly any possessions or savings to speak of, but after spending just a few minutes with the lawyer, I realized that a will was about so much more than just money.

My husband and I were suddenly faced with the decision of where our daughter (and future children) would live if we passed away. We had to decide who would be in charge of their money and if there were any special instructions for future parenting decisions. It was something we had never talked about, but it was a very important decision we had to make. Without a will, grandparents or our siblings could have fought each other for custody of our children. A simple piece of paper solved a host of potential issues.

When we chose our Power of Attorneys, we had to answer tough questions about our end of life choices and who would manage our finances and our health decisions if we were incapable of doing so ourselves. It was scary and overwhelming, but when it was all over and everything was finalised, I felt like a weight had been lifted off my shoulders. While I had never given my death or a possible debilitating illness any real thought, knowing that everything was planned and taken care of gave me tremendous peace of mind.

As soon as we got our paperwork handed to us, we immediately purchased an inexpensive fire-proof safe to keep it in. We also put in our birth and marriage certificates and photocopies of our passports, social insurance numbers, and drivers licenses inside. We made hard copies of all our digital photos and documents and stored those inside the safe as well! It was a small and simple purchase, but that fire-proof safe makes me totally feel like a real grown-up!

≫

LOOK AT ME!
I'M ADULTING ALL OVER THE PLACE!

≪

We also decided to get life insurance. Some people thought we were too young, or that it was "morbid" to get life insurance in our mid twenties, but I totally disagree. Most people have car and home insurance, but that doesn't mean they are expecting or "causing" their homes to burn down. Having insurance ensures that, if something horrible were to happen, we would have the financial means to replace our home or fix our car. Our life insurance money would take care of our children's secondary education and make sure that our loved ones wouldn't have to pay unforeseen expenses out of their own pockets if we should pass on. If just my husband or I were to pass away without the other, our life insurance policies would allow the remaining spouse to take time off work to grieve and support the children, without having to worry about lost wages.

One last thing that I think is really important is to have a password tracker that loved ones can access if they need to. Place this in a safe spot, like your safe, and make sure that someone knows where to find it in case of an emergency. This will allow your loved ones the ability to pay your bills and take care of your affairs if you are not capable. You will find a **Password Log** in this chapter.

So, while no one wants to think about death, illnesses or zombies, it's important that we are prepared. Protect your future right now by taking a few minutes to fill out the pages in this chapter!

Family Emergency Guide

OUR FAMILY CONTACT INFORMATION

Address: _____ Home Phone: _____

Name: _____ Cell Phone: _____

Name: _____ Cell Phone: _____

PRIMARY EMERGENCY CONTACT

Name: _____ Cell Number: _____

Address: _____

SECONDARY EMERGENCY CONTACT

Name: _____ Cell Number: _____

Address: _____

INSURANCE INFORMATION

Provider: _____ Phone: _____

Policy/Group Number: _____

OTHER IMPORTANT INFORMATION

Emergency Meet-Up Location: _____

Other Information: _____

_____

PEDIATRICIAN

OTHER DOCTORS

DENTIST

HOSPITAL

MEDICATION

URGENT

Emergency Contact List

NAME	PHONE	DETAILS

Safety First

CHECK OFF THE FOLLOWING LIST TO ENSURE YOUR HOME IS SAFE.

O **Smoke Alarms**
  At least one on every floor.

O **Carbon Monoxide Detectors**
  At least one on every floor.

O **Fire Extinguisher**
  One in kitchen & one by furnace, hot water heater, or dryer.

O **Electrical Outlets**
  Do not overload.

O **Water Heater**
  Don't forget to do a yearly inspection.

O **Windows**
  Make sure they can easily open.

O **Dryer**
  Clean vent hose yearly.

O **Emergency Kit**
  Check expiration dates and make sure supplies are in working condition.

O **Emergency Plan/Binder**
  Check yearly to make sure documents & contacts are up to date.

O **Family Binder**
  Check yearly to make sure documents & contacts are up to date.

O **First Aid Kit**
  Make sure to check expiration dates and to refill missing supplies.

O **Spare Key to House Hidden Outside**
  Evaluate the location of hidden key and check occasionally to see if key is missing.

Emergency Checklist

NEED TO KNOW

Family Meet-Up Location: _____

Evacuation Plan: _____

_____

_____

_____

_____

_____

_____

BASIC SURVIVAL SUPPLIES

- ○ Water: 3–5 Gallons Stored
- ○ Flashlight for Each Family Member
- ○ Battery Powered Radio
- ○ Important Papers/Docs
- ○ Sleeping Bag
- ○ Poncho
- ○ Extra Batteries
- ○ 72-Hour Supply of Food

- ○ Candles/Headlamps
- ○ Pocket Knife
- ○ Hatchet/Axe
- ○ Sewing Kit
- ○ Duct Tape
- ○ Cash: At Least $40
- ○ 1 Full Outfit for Each Family Member

SANITATION

- ○ Toilet Paper + Tissues
- ○ Comb/Brush
- ○ Toothbrush/Toothpaste
- ○ Hand Sanitizer + Soap
- ○ First Aid Kit
- ○ Trash Bags

EXTRA STUFF

- ○ Sunscreen
- ○ Pet Food/Supplies
- ○ Camping Gear
- ○ Kids Go Kit
- ○ _____
- ○ _____

Place your survival supplies in a location that is easily accessible so you can get to your items in an emergency.

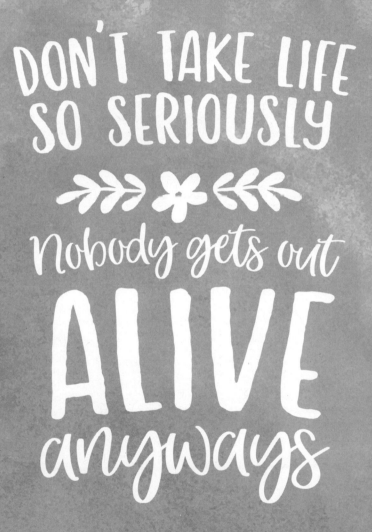

Password log

ACCOUNT:	SIGN IN:	PASSWORD:

Adulting 101
A CHECKLIST FOR GROWN UPS

WILL
Having a will is about more than just who receives your belongings after you pass. A will can make your end-of-life decisions known and it is crucial when deciding who will raise your children in your absence.

POWER OF ATTORNEY
Choose a close friend or family member you trust to take care of your financial and medical decisions if you are unable to do so.

FIRE-PROOF SAFE
A small and inexpensive safe is all you need to ensure that your important documents are protected. You can also store photocopies of your identification and digital copies of your photographs in your safe.

LIFE INSURANCE
Even a small amount of life insurance can go a long way to ensuring that your loved ones are taken care of, or at least not faced with unexpected costs if you should suddenly pass away.

EMERGENCY SAVINGS ACCOUNT
You must have a savings account with a minimum of three months salary to protect you and your family in case of job loss or unexpected expenses.

≋ Chapter Nine ≋

ORGANIZING FOR FUN

HOW TO MAKE THE MOST OF EACH AND EVERY MOMENT.

When it comes to our free time, most of us want to the opposite of our strict and planned work schedule. We opt instead to leisurely enjoy ourselves when we are not at work, rarely structuring or scheduling this time. The result of this laid-back approach to our free time is we rarely get to do the activities we actually want to, and instead, spend our precious time off staring at the television screen or surfing the web.

For years, "planning" my free time involved choosing what restaurant to eat at or choosing which movie to watch. Sometimes, I would meet a friend for a coffee date or take some time to go shopping on the weekends. Wild and adventurous, I know. My workweek was so full of never-ending to-dos, I looked forward to having the weekends off to do "nothing." And that is exactly what I usually did...*nothing*.

≫≫

WHILE THE IDEA OF SPENDING MY FREE TIME CRUSHING NETFLIX OR STALKING RANDOM ACQUAINTANCES ON FACEBOOK SOUNDED AWESOME, THE REALITY WAS THAT IT LEFT ME FEELING REALLY UNHAPPY AND UNFULFILLED.

≪≪

Why was I was no longer painting, crafting, or enjoying weekend road trips with my family? These are the things that I really *longed* for, the things that really made my heart sing. Why was I not spending my free time engaging in activities that brought me joy or spending time with the people I love? My answer was, of course, was that I just didn't have the time.

IT'S NOT ABOUT "HAVING" TIME IT'S ABOUT "MAKING" IT.

The truth is, we need to "make time" each and every day for the things and people we love. In order to do this, we have to work "free time" into our schedules and we have to plan *how* we are going to spend that time. **I'm not some militant taskmaster who plans every minute of every day, but it's those days when I have *nothing* planned that I always regret not doing or seeing more.**

As much as it pains me to admit it, the weekends that I love the most are the ones where I get up early and seize the day. When I fill my free time with crafting, family fun, and some occasional adventure, I feel energized and exhilarated. When I spend my weekend laying around and watching non-stop television, I feel tired and lethargic. I need to step out of my comfort zone, and my pajamas, in order to make the most of my time off from work.

When we fail to manage our free time properly, we waste it. With most of our time on this earth dedicated to either work or sleep, the time we have to do what we truly enjoy should be the last thing we waste. Let's say the average person lives to be seventy-five years of age and sleeps an average eight hours per night. That equals a whooping 33 percent of your life spent sleeping! On workdays, 50 percent of your waking hours are spent working at your job—half of your entire day. With just that precious ⅓ of your life remaining, you still need to make time to eat, drive, shop, do housework and care for your loved ones. When we really think about, the time we have in life to dedicate to our own happiness is a very, very small amount.

So how can you make the most of your time off? How can you find more time for the things and people you love the most? A little planning of course!

You may be skeptical. Maybe you actually **love** the idea of spending your weekends relaxing and escaping from your structured routine. Let me assure you, you can still have relaxed and unstructured leisure time, even while planning some fun.

Make a list of all the movies you want to see, books you want to read, and local places that you would love to visit. These lists will come in handy when you have a few free hours to kill on a Saturday afternoon and need a bit of inspiration.

Get your family involved in writing down all the various activities that you could do together for "family fun" time and schedule just one or two hours every week to check something off that list. When I first made our list with my kids, it was so sweet to hear their wonderful ideas of how we could spend more time together. I thought they would suggest really extreme and expensive activities, but instead, they suggested going for bike rides and doing crafts together. I realized what they really wanted was just quality time, no matter what we did together.

I also want you to really think about the things that make you happy and create yourself a "happy hobby list" filled with all the things that you would love to do if only you had the time to do them. Maybe you want to play golf more often or learn to play guitar. This list should include the things you already love doing and some things that you have always wanted to try.

Now, let's pick something. Just by picking one movie from your list to watch or spending a few hours one night for a "family game night" with your kids when you get home from work will go a long way to increasing your happiness. Take a few hours on a Saturday morning to work on a hobby that makes you happy, instead of surfing the web or watching some boring television show. Don't forget to also make time to call your mother for Pete's sake!

»»»

I'M NOT SUGGESTING THAT YOU PLAN AND SCHEDULE EVERY SINGLE MOMENT OF YOUR FREE TIME. JUST BY SPENDING A FEW HOURS A WEEK ON THINGS THAT BRING YOU JOY, YOU CAN DRASTICALLY IMPROVE YOUR OVERALL HAPPINESS.

«««

I now make crafting a priority in my life! I schedule some much-needed bonding time for just me and my hot glue gun at least once a week. I also schedule both a "family game night" and a "family movie night" each and every week with our little family of five. We all take turns choosing board games and movies and these nights are, by far, the most cherished part of my week.

I also always plan our family vacations. In the past, I took a more laid-back approach to our vacations, choosing to "play things by ear" instead of planning all of the details in advance. Our first trip to Disney World was all I needed to see the error of my ways. You HAVE to plan your Disney vacation. An unplanned Disney trip equals long lines and missed fun; I had to learn this the hard way.

A trip to Disney World is pretty much the epitome of why it is so important to plan your leisure time. Those who plan their day at the park avoid long lines, get to see all of their favorite Disney characters, and can enjoy the park at their own relaxed and stress-free pace. They also get front row seats for both the parades and the fireworks.

Those of us who don't plan the park spend hours in the hot sun waiting to ride a freaking teacup, never see a single princess, and totally miss the parade because we are stuck behind masses of people trampling each other for a glimpse of the mouse.

Obviously, Disney is an extreme case, but the lesson can really be applied to all vacations and even our leisure time in general. A little planning can really make the most of every minute.

In this chapter, you will find a complete **travel-planning worksheets,** which you can use to plan your next vacation efficiently, and even your "someday" dream vacations too. I adore these worksheets and I use them for every trip we take, whether we are traveling for a few weeks at a time, or just a few days. These worksheets have everything you need for the perfect vacation, from a packing list to a full itinerary checklist.

I have also included lists for books to read, movies to watch, family fun ideas, date night ideas, and of course, your favorite happy hobbies! Just take a few minutes to fill out these lists and then commit to choosing one or two of these things each and every week. Your free time should be quality time, so make it a priority in your life.

I will get you started by sharing some of my family's favorite kid-friendly "family fun night" ideas and some grown-up "date night" ideas that Joe and I love to do together!

FAMILY FUN NIGHT:

- **Homemade Pizza Party**
- **Fondue Night**
- **Water Gun Fight**
- **Going on a Hike**
- **Family Book Club**
- **Dance Party**
- **Make a Giant Blanket Fort**
- **DIY Ice Cream Sundaes**

- **Board Game Night**
- **Movie and Popcorn**
- **Campfire and S'mores**
- **Baking Dessert Together**
- **Family Bike Ride**
- **Playing at the Park**
- **Play Hide and Seek Together**
- **Karaoke Night at Home**

DATE NIGHT IDEAS:

- Go for a Hike
- Batting Cages
- Ride Go-Karts
- Visit an Art Gallery
- Watch a Play
- Have Drinks at a Bar
- Just Go for a Long Drive in the Car and Talk
- Wine Tasting Tour
- Local Panic Room
- Couples Cooking Class
- Dinner and a Movie
- Play Mini Golf
- Go Bowling
- Visit a Museum
- Visit a Comedy Club
- Pack a Picnic and Stargaze

Someday, when we are old and grey, we are not going to wish we would have spent more time watching television or reading the status updates of people we don't even like on Facebook. We are going to wish that we had traveled more, spent more time with loved ones, and that we made time for our dreams and passions. Time flies by so fast, let's not waste a single second of it. So what are you waiting for? Plan some fun right now!

≫

TAKE TIME TO DO WHAT MAKES YOUR SOUL HAPPY.

≪

Take time to
do what makes
♥
your soul
happy

Books to Read

Movies to Watch

Date Night Ideas

Happy Hobby List

LIST ALL THE HOBBIES YOU LOVE
(OR WOULD LOVE TO TRY)

Family Time

IS SACRED TIME & SHOULD BE

PROTECTED

and

RESPECTED

Family Fun Night Ideas

- ○ _____
- ○ _____
- ○ _____
- ○ _____
- ○ _____
- ○ _____
- ○ _____
- ○ _____
- ○ _____
- ○ _____
- ○ _____
- ○ _____
- ○ _____

Pre-Travel To-Dos

PART 1

4-6 MONTHS

- ○ _____
- ○ _____
- ○ _____
- ○ _____
- ○ _____
- ○ _____
- ○ _____

1-3 MONTHS

- ○ _____
- ○ _____
- ○ _____
- ○ _____
- ○ _____
- ○ _____
- ○ _____

2 WEEKS

- ○ _____
- ○ _____
- ○ _____
- ○ _____
- ○ _____
- ○ _____
- ○ _____

Pre-Travel To-Dos

PART 2

1 WEEK

○ _____
○ _____
○ _____
○ _____
○ _____
○ _____
○ _____

THE DAY BEFORE

○ _____
○ _____
○ _____
○ _____
○ _____
○ _____
○ _____

THE DAY OF

○ _____
○ _____
○ _____
○ _____
○ _____
○ _____
○ _____

❧ Travel Details ❧

WHERE? _____   WHEN? _____

WITH WHO? _____

FLIGHT 1

Airport: _____   Airline: _____
Flight number: _____   Boarding info: _____
Departure date: _____   Departure time: _____
Arrival date: _____   Arrival date: _____

FLIGHT 2

Airport: _____   Airline: _____
Flight number: _____   Boarding info: _____
Departure date: _____   Departure time: _____
Arrival date: _____   Arrival date: _____

CRUISE

Cruise line: _____   Cruise ship: _____
Port location: _____   Notes: _____
To sea date: _____   Departure time: _____   _____
To port date: _____   Arrival time: _____   _____

HOTEL 1

Name: _____   Phone: _____
Address: _____   Check-in time: _____
_____   Check-out time: _____
Notes: _____

HOTEL 2

Name: _____   Phone: _____
Address: _____   Check-in time: _____
_____   Check-out time: _____
Notes: _____

VEHICLE 1

Rental company: _____   Phone: _____
Vehicle requested: _____
Pick-up /   Date: _____   Time: _____   Location: _____
Drop-off /   Date: _____   Time: _____   Location: _____
Notes: _____

OTHER

Name: _____   Phone: _____
Address: _____   Date: _____   Time: _____
Notes: _____

Travel Expenses

BEFORE TRIP

	BUDGET	ACTUAL
Travel agent	____	____
Luggage	____	____
Clothes/Shoes/Accessories	____	____
Personal care items	____	____
Passports	____	____
Travel insurance	____	____
Reading material	____	____
Other leisure	____	____
Home/Child/Pet care	____	____
_____	____	____
_____	____	____
_____	____	____
_____	____	____
_____	____	____
_____	____	____
SUBTOTAL	____	____

LODGING

	BUDGET	ACTUAL
Hotel/Motel/Campsite	____	____
Cruise:	____	____
All-inclusive	____	____
Gratuity	____	____
_____	____	____
_____	____	____
SUBTOTAL	____	____

FOOD/DRINK

	BUDGET	ACTUAL
Dining out	____	____
Room service	____	____
Gratuity	____	____
Groceries	____	____
Snacks	____	____
Beverages - non-alcoholic	____	____
Beverages - alcoholic	____	____
_____	____	____
_____	____	____
SUBTOTAL	____	____

ENTERTAINMENT

	BUDGET	ACTUAL
Shopping	____	____
Souvenirs	____	____
Guided tours	____	____
Amusement parks	____	____
Museums	____	____
Water activities	____	____
Spa/Salon	____	____
Bars/Nightlife	____	____
Gambling	____	____
_____	____	____
_____	____	____
_____	____	____
_____	____	____
SUBTOTAL	____	____

TRANSPORTATION

	BUDGET	ACTUAL
Airfare & related expenses	____	____
Shuttle service	____	____
Parking	____	____
Vehicle rental	____	____
Fuel	____	____
Tolls	____	____
Public transportation	____	____
_____	____	____
_____	____	____
SUBTOTAL	____	____

GRAND TOTAL   **BUDGET:**   **ACTUAL:**

Vacation Ideas

STATES

ATTRACTIONS

ACTIVITIES

COUNTRIES

BEACHES

MOUNTAINS

RESORTS

HOTELS

ALL-INCLUSIVES

TOURS

CRUISES

FESTIVALS

RESTAURANTS

TRAVEL AGENTS

OTHER

Packing List

CLOTHING

- ○ T-shirts
- ○ Sweaters
- ○ Blouses
- ○ Pants
- ○ Shorts
- ○ Dresses
- ○ Suits
- ○ Ties
- ○ Workout
- ○ Bathing Suits
- ○ _____
- ○ _____

OUTERWEAR

- ○ Hats
- ○ Jackets
- ○ Gloves
- ○ _____
- ○ _____
- ○ _____
- ○ _____

UNDERGARMENTS

- ○ Pajamas
- ○ Socks
- ○ Underwear
- ○ Bras
- ○ Camisoles
- ○ _____
- ○ _____

SHOES

- ○ Running shoes
- ○ Dress shoes
- ○ Sandals
- ○ Flip Flops
- ○ Boots
- ○ _____
- ○ _____

TOILETRIES

- ○ Shampoo/Conditioner
- ○ Toothpaste/Toothbrush
- ○ Floss
- ○ Hair Products
- ○ Hair Dryer
- ○ Curling/Flat Iron
- ○ Hair Accessories
- ○ Soap
- ○ Lotion
- ○ Deodorant
- ○ Face Wash/Cream
- ○ Makeup
- ○ Cotton Swabs
- ○ Feminine Products
- ○ Nail Accessories
- ○ Medications
- ○ First Aid Kit
- ○ _____
- ○ _____
- ○ _____

EXTRAS

- ○ Sunglasses
- ○ Belts
- ○ Jewelery
- ○ Sunscreen
- ○ Insect Repellent
- ○ _____
- ○ _____
- ○ _____
- ○ _____
- ○ _____

DOCUMENTS

- ○ Passport
- ○ ID
- ○ Boarding Passes
- ○ Reservation Information
- ○ Itinerary
- ○ Travel Insurance
- ○ Emergency Contact
- ○ Information
- ○ Money
- ○ Credit Cards
- ○ _____
- ○ _____
- ○ _____
- ○ _____
- ○ _____

ELECTRONICS

- ○ Cell Phone
- ○ Tablet
- ○ Laptop
- ○ Camera
- ○ Chargers
- ○ Extra Batteries
- ○ _____
- ○ _____

Places To...

SEE

STAY

SHOP

EAT

OTHER

❧ Daily Itinerary ❧

DATE: / /

MORNING: _____
_____
_____

AFTERNOON: _____
_____
_____

NIGHT: _____
_____
_____

DATE: / /

MORNING: _____
_____
_____

AFTERNOON: _____
_____
_____

NIGHT: _____
_____
_____

DATE: / /

MORNING: _____
_____
_____

AFTERNOON: _____
_____
_____

NIGHT: _____
_____
_____

DATE: / /

MORNING: _____
_____
_____

AFTERNOON: _____
_____
_____

NIGHT: _____
_____
_____

NOTES: _____
_____
_____

≋ Chapter Ten ≋

LABELING IS MAGIC

HOW TO LABEL EVERYTHING LIKE A WEIRDO (AND KEEP YOUR HOME ORGANIZED FOR GOOD).

The one question I get asked more than any other is definitely, "How do I get my family to pick up after themselves?" It can be really frustrating when you work your butt off trying to keep your home clean and organized, but the rest of your family hasn't seemed to have gotten the memo. No one wants to be constantly cleaning up after their messy loved ones. Living as the family maid can cause hurt feelings and resentment, and it can also cause us to lash out at the ones we love (just ask my poor husband).

While there isn't some amazing secret recipe that can transform your family into organized clean freaks, there is a way to make sure they put their things away **most** of the time. You have probably guessed by the title of this chapter, but yeah, it's good old-fashioned labels. Labeling is legit magic you guys! It actually drastically changes the way we put away our belongings on a subconscious level.

To ensure that labeling is really effective, it's important that we follow the S.P.A.C.E. organizing method first (described in Chapter Four, Organizing Your Home). Once you have sorted, purged, assigned, and contained your belongings, now comes the fun part...labeling! You took the time to create those "homes" for all your stuff, now pretty labels will make sure everything finds its way back to those homes when you are done using it.

Not only does labeling give you the ability to really personalize the look of your organizational system with custom colors and patterns, it is critical in ensuring that everyone (including you) can find and put away things with ease.

Hi. My name is Cas and I'm a labeling addict. I'll admit it, I may go a tad overboard with the labels in my home. I label everything! I have labels in my fridge, in every closet and drawer and I even label the toilet paper basket in my linen closet (despite being able to clearly see the rolls inside). The downside to my obsession with labeling is that I can come across like a bit like a nutter to company, but you can keep your labels just for those hidden areas inside cabinets and closets if you like. The reason I'm so gaga for labels? They stop me and the rest of my family from shoving our belongings here, there, and EVERYWHERE, making everything messy and cluttered. Without labels, all of my hard work cleaning and organizing my home would be for nothing.

Let's face it, we are all a little lazy sometimes and we all have the tendency to just put stuff away wherever it seems to fit. Before my obsession with labeling, I would organize and reorganize my home, just to have it look like a disaster again a few weeks later. No one, not even myself, was putting things back in the proper homes.

One of my BIGGEST pet peeves used to be that I could never find the condiments in our fridge. It may seem like a pretty petty thing to stress about, but every single day we would have to route and hunt through our fridge for the ketchup. We would often have two or three open bottles of ketchup on the go at once and STILL we would have to rummage through the fridge to find them. I tried implementing the "condiments go in the door of the fridge" rule, but despite my constant nagging, no one ever remembered. Heck, even I forgot my own rule and would toss the ketchup back into the fridge without a second thought.

One day, after looking through my fridge for the hundredth time, I made a big, fat label that said "CONDIMENTS" and taped it inside the door of the fridge where I wanted to the condiments to go. Guess what? We have **never** had to search for the ketchup again. That label is the simple reminder we needed and whether it is subconscious or not, everyone **always** puts the condiments back in the door now... without having to be told.

All over the world, companies large and small use the 5S or CANDO (Cleaning up, Arranging, Neatness, Discipline, and Ongoing improvement) method for maintaining clean and organized work spaces. Basically, these methods are just systems set in place so everything is kept neat and organized through visual reminders. What the heck are these visual reminders? Yep, that's right: labels. You have probably seen this method in action before, with outlines marked where each tool belongs, tape on the factory floor or everything from safety procedures to the garbage cans clearly labeled. The reason companies like Apple, Ford Motors, Hewlett-Packard, Harley Davidson, and countless others are bananas for labeling is because they really work. They motivate employees to clean up after themselves and put things back where they belong, without having to say a single word.

So yes, not only can you make your home look more organized (and pretty) with some beautiful custom labels, but you can also transform it into a super functional and efficient organizing machine with the labels found in this book (and get your family to actually put their things away properly).

Grab some scissors and go ahead and cut the labels out of the book and use them throughout your home (or download your free printables and use those). You can protect your labels by laminating them or using clear contact paper—even using some clear packing tape works in a pinch!

Your crazy labeling is going to seem, well...**crazy** at first. I bought my first label maker about five years ago and I lost my mind and labeled everything in my home, I actually even labeled my label maker (that was perhaps a bit much). I was just so amazed at how these tiny pieces of paper could motivate my entire family to keep things tidy. People who came to visit used to constantly crack jokes about the obnoxious amounts of labels everywhere, but now almost every single one of my friends and family are labeling junkies too (who's laughing now?). They have all seen the light!

So, get to labeling your condiments people! I have included labels for your fridge, pantry, linen closet, office, paperwork, toys and of course blank labels so you can label your home any way you choose! **The one thing you can never have too many of is definitely labels!**

Pantry Labels

1½" x 3¾" Labels

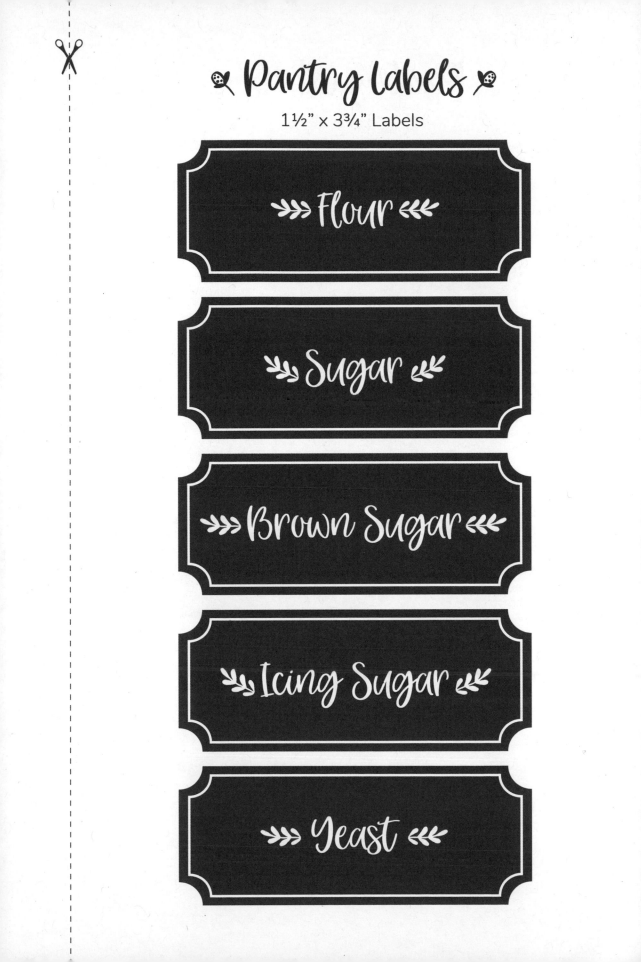

Flour

Sugar

Brown Sugar

Icing Sugar

Yeast

Pantry Labels

1½" x 3¾" Labels

- Corn Flour
- Corn Starch
- Cocoa
- Baking Soda
- Baking Powder

Pantry Labels

1½" x 3¾" Labels

Oats

Chocolate Chips

Bread Crumbs

Crackers

Cookies

Pantry Labels

1½" x 3¾" Labels

Pasta

Rice

Beans

Cereal

Trail Mix

Pantry Labels

1½" x 3¾" Labels

Popcorn

Coffee

Tea

Hot Chocolate

Pancake Mix

Spice Labels

1½" Round Labels

ALLSPICE

ALMOND EXTRACT

BASIL

CARAWAY

CARDAMON

CHILI POWDER

CHIVES

CILANTRO

CINNAMON

CLOVES

CORIANDER

CREAM OF TARTAR

CUMIN

CURRY POWDER

DILL

Spice Labels

1½" Round Labels

GARLIC

GINGER

LEMON PEPPER

MUSTARD SEEDS

NUTMEG

ONION POWDER

OREGANO

PAPRIKA

PARSLEY

PEPPER

ROSEMARY

SALT

SESAME SEEDS

THYME

TURMERIC

Bathroom Labels for Jars

3" × 2½" and ¾" × 2½" Labels

Bath Salts

Bubble Bath

BATH SALTS

BUBBLE BATH

Cotton Balls

Cotton Pads

COTTON BALLS

COTTON PADS

Bathroom Labels for Jars

3" x 2½", ¾" x 2½" and Blank Labels

Cotton Swabs

Sponges

COTTON SWABS

SPONGES

Bathroom Labels for Baskets

2½" x 4" Labels

Allergy

Digestive RX

Dental

Bathroom Labels for Baskets

2½" x 4" Labels

Feminine Hygiene

First Aid

Hair

Bathroom Labels for Baskets

2½" x 4" Labels

Hers

His

Hair

Bathroom Labels for Baskets

2½" x 4" Labels

Kids

Lotions

Makeup

Bathroom Labels for Baskets

2½" x 4" Labels

Medicine

Nails

Pain Relievers

Bathroom Labels for Baskets

2½" x 4" Labels

Shaving

Sunscreen &
Insect Repellent

Toilet Paper

Bathroom Labels for Baskets

2½" x 4" Labels

Toiletries

Vitamins

Extra Products

Office Labels for Baskets

2½" x 4" Labels

Cords & Cables

File Folders

Labels

Office Labels for Baskets

2½" x 4" Labels

Notebooks

Office Supplies

Paper

Office Labels for Baskets

2½" x 4" Labels

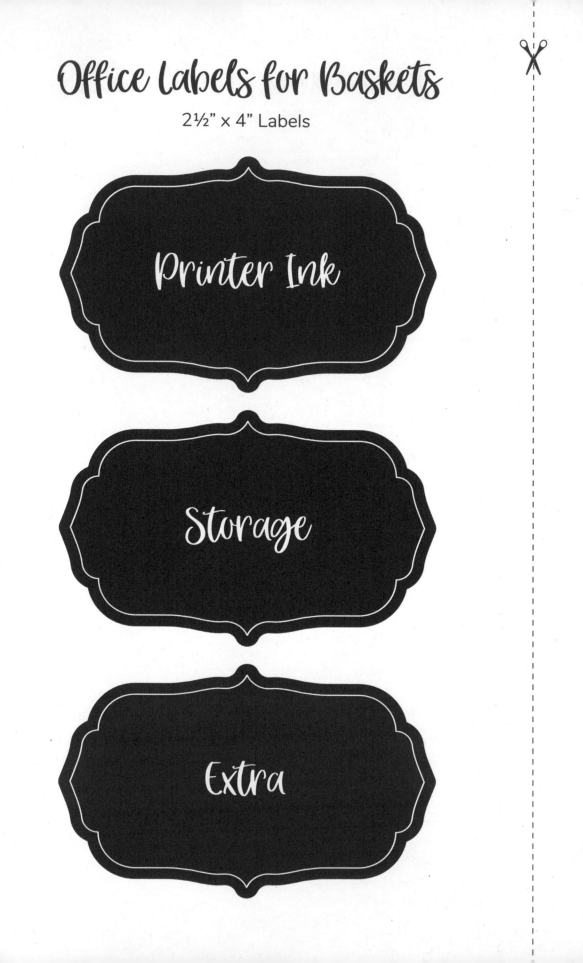

Printer Ink

Storage

Extra

Hanging File Folder Labels

½" x 2" Tab Inserts for Hanging File Folder

ACTION	TAXES
TO BE PAID	TO DO
TO FILE	TO READ
BANK STATEMENTS	BENEFITS
CREDIT CARD STATEMENTS	HEALTH
INSURANCE	INVESTMENTS
LEGAL	MANUALS
MORTGAGE	PETS
PHOTOCOPIES OF ID	RECEIPTS
TRAVEL	UTILITIES
VEHICLE	WARRANTIES

Kid Toy Labels

2½" x 4" Labels

BLOCKS

BOOKS

CARS & TRUCKS

Kid Toy Labels

2½" x 4" Labels

CRAFTS

DRESS UP

DOLLS

Kid Toy Labels

2½" x 4" Labels

GAMES

LEGOS

MUSIC

Kid Toy Labels

2½" x 4" Labels

PLAY FOOD

PLAY SETS

PUZZLES

Kid Toy Labels

2½" x 4" Labels

SPORTS

STUFFED ANIMALS

SUPER HEROES

Fridge Labels

1½" x 3¾" Labels

Cheese

Condiments

Dairy

Drinks

Eggs

Fridge Labels

1½" x 3¾" Labels

Fruits

Meats

Salad Dressing

Sauces

Syrups

Fridge Labels

1½" x 3¾" Labels

Veggies

Yogurt

Leftovers

Lunches

Miscellaneous

Laundry Labels
2½" x 4" Labels

Baking Soda

Borax

Detergent

Laundry Labels

2½" x 4" Labels

Fabric Softener

Stain Remover

Washing Soda

Linen Closet Labels

2½" x 4" Labels

Beach Towels

Blankets

Crib Sheets

Linen Closet Labels

2½" x 4" Labels

Double Sheets

Duvet Covers

Hand Towels

Linen Closet Labels

2½" x 4" Labels

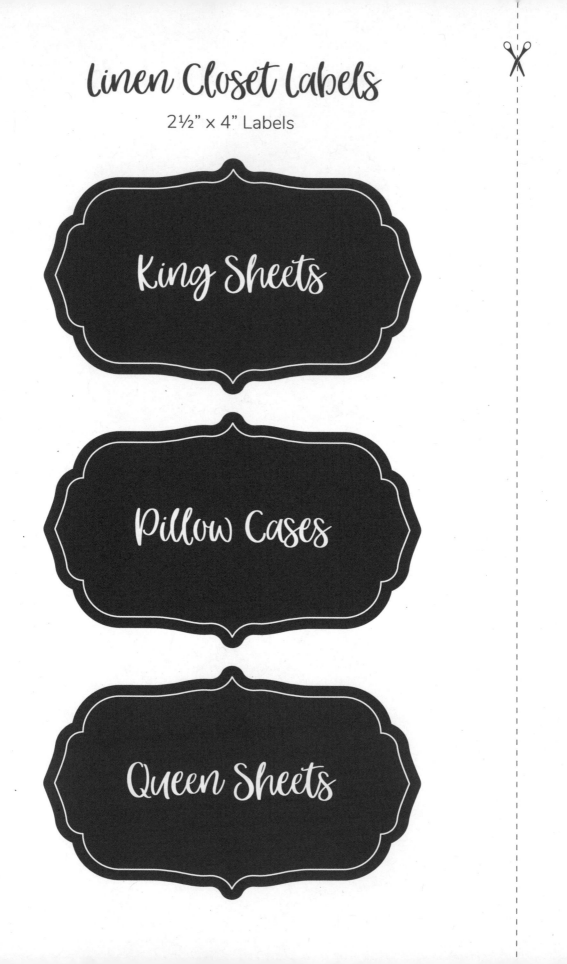

King Sheets

Pillow Cases

Queen Sheets

Linen Closet Labels

2½" x 4" Labels

Towels

Twin Sheets

Wash Cloths

Crafts Labels

2½" x 4" Labels

≫≫ Adhesives ≪≪

≫≫ Beads ≪≪

≫≫ Brushes ≪≪

❧ Crafts Labels ☙

2½" x 4" Labels

>>> Candle Making <<<

>>> Clay <<<

>>> Embellishments <<<

Crafts Labels

2½" x 4" Labels

Fabric

Felt

Gift Tags

Crafts Labels

2½" x 4" Labels

Glitter

Glue

Jewelery

Crafts Labels

2½" x 4" Labels

Kid's Crafts

Markers

Paint

Crafts Labels

2½" x 4" Labels

❦ Crafts Labels ❦

2½" x 4" Labels

Ribbon

Scissors

Scrapbooking

Crafts Labels

2½" x 4" Labels

Crafts Labels

2½" x 4" Labels

Tape

Thread

Tissue Paper

Crafts Labels

2½" x 4" Labels

⋙ Tools ⋘

⋙ Tulle ⋘

⋙ Washi Tape ⋘

ACKNOWLEDGMENTS

To Joe, for teaching me how to "adult" when I thought all hope was lost for me. You continue to be my life's compass, always leading me in the right direction. Your endless love and support has gifted me with the most incredible life and I am so grateful and blessed to have you as my husband. You've made me whole and I love you.

To my amazing little humans, Izzy, Abby, and Milo, I am so proud to be your mom. You fill me with such joy and love and you are always my biggest cheerleaders. You three are what drive me to be a better mom, wife, business owner, and overall human being.

To my ClutterBug followers—I love you guys. You have no idea how much your kind comments and continued support mean to me. Every morning, the first thing I do when I wake up is read your wonderful messages and comments. You guys brighten my day and totally give me my purpose in life. I can't find the words to describe how important each and every one of you are to me, so I will just say—thank you.

I have to give a shout out to my publisher, Mango. The entire Mango team is so talented, professional, but most of all, supportive. You have held my hand, step-by-step, to make my dream of becoming an author a reality. Working with you all has been an absolute joy and I can't thank you enough for taking a chance on me.

And lastly, to the incredible Alice A. Jones, I am so lucky to have you in my life. I can never thank you enough for the beautiful design work you have done in this book and on my blog. I'm always blown away by your talent and your ability to "read my mind" when it comes to everything you create. I cannot wait for the rest of the world to discover your incredible gifts and give you the credit you deserve. Don't forget about me when you're hella famous Alice.

ABOUT THE AUTHOR

Cassandra Aarssen is a Professional Organizer, author, and the recovering super-slob behind the successful organizing business, ClutterBug. In her efforts to transform herself from a super-slob to a clean freak, she has created a successful career as an organizing expert through her YouTube channel, blog, podcast, and her best-selling book *Real Life Organizing*. Cassandra's organizing and decluttering advice and tips have been featured on Oprah.com, *The Marilyn Denis Show*, *Popular Science* magazine, and *Better Homes and Gardens*. When she isn't working on ridding the world of clutter, she spends her free time with her family in Ontario, Canada.